THE LIFE RECOVERY®

WORKBOOK FOR

Eating Disorders

A Bible-Centered Approach for Taking Your Life Back

STEPHEN ARTERBURN & DAV

D1501688

Tyndale House Publishers
Carol Stream, Illinois

Visit Tyndale online at www.liferecoverybible.com and www.tyndale.com.

TYNDALE, Tyndale's quill logo, and *Life Recovery* are registered trademarks of Tyndale House Publishers.

The Big Book is a registered trademark of A.A. World Services, Inc.

The Life Recovery Workbook for Eating Disorders: A Bible-Centered Approach for Taking Your Life Back

Cover design by Dan Farrell

Edited by Ellen Richard Vosburg

The author is represented by the literary agency of Alive Literary Agency, 7680 Goddard Street, Suite 200, Colorado Springs, CO 80920, www.aliveliterary.com.

Unless otherwise indicated, all Scripture quotations are taken from the *Holy Bible,* New Living Translation, copyright © 1996, 2004, 2015 by Tyndale House Foundation. Used by permission of Tyndale House Publishers, Carol Stream, Illinois 60188. All rights reserved.

Scripture quotations marked KJV are taken from the *Holy Bible,* King James Version.

Scripture quotations marked TLB are taken from *The Living Bible,* copyright © 1971 by Tyndale House Foundation. Used by permission of Tyndale House Publishers, Carol Stream, Illinois 60188. All rights reserved.

Scripture quotations marked MSG are taken from *THE MESSAGE,* copyright © 1993, 2002, 2018 by Eugene H. Peterson. Used by permission of NavPress. All rights reserved. Represented by Tyndale House Publishers.

Scripture quotations marked NASB are taken from the New American Standard Bible,® copyright © 1960, 1962, 1963, 1968, 1971, 1972, 1973, 1975, 1977, 1995 by The Lockman Foundation. Used by permission.

Scripture quotations marked NIV are taken from the Holy Bible, *New International Version,*® *NIV.*® Copyright © 1973, 1978, 1984, 2011 by Biblica, Inc.® Used by permission. All rights reserved worldwide.

The brief excerpts from Alcoholics Anonymous and the Twelve Steps are reprinted and adapted with permission of Alcoholics Anonymous World Services, Inc. Permission to reprint and adapt the Twelve Steps does not mean that AAWS has reviewed or approved the contents of this publication, or that AAWS necessarily agrees with the views expressed herein. A.A. is a program of recovery from alcoholism only—use of the Twelve Steps in connection with programs and activities which are patterned after A.A., but which address other problems, or in any other non-A.A. context, does not imply otherwise. Additionally, while A.A. is a spiritual program, A.A. is not a religious program. Thus, A.A. is not affiliated or allied with any sect, denomination, or specific religious belief.

The profiles in this workbook are composite characteristics of persons who have had the courage to work the steps on various issues in their lives and on their own addictive behaviors. Names, ages, and situations have been modified to protect their anonymity.

For information about special discounts for bulk purchases, please contact Tyndale House Publishers at csresponse@tyndale.com, or call 1-800-323-9400.

ISBN 978-1-4964-4211-6

Printed in the United States of America

26	25	24	23	22	21	20
7	6	5	4	3	2	1

This workbook is dedicated to every fellow struggler who has had the courage to face the truth about themselves, the humility to abandon their flawed attempts at living, and the willingness to find God's truth and live accordingly.

CONTENTS

The Twelve Steps of Alcoholics Anonymous

1. We admitted we were powerless over alcohol—that our lives had become unmanageable.
2. Came to believe that a Power greater than ourselves could restore us to sanity.
3. Made a decision to turn our will and our lives over to the care of God *as we understood Him.*
4. Made a searching and fearless moral inventory of ourselves.
5. Admitted to God, to ourselves, and to another human being the exact nature of our wrongs.
6. Were entirely ready to have God remove all these defects of character.
7. Humbly asked Him to remove our shortcomings.
8. Made a list of all persons we had harmed, and became willing to make amends to them all.
9. Made direct amends to such people wherever possible, except when to do so would injure them or others.
10. Continued to take personal inventory and when we were wrong promptly admitted it.
11. Sought through prayer and meditation to improve our conscious contact with God *as we understood Him*, praying only for knowledge of His will for us and the power to carry that out.
12. Having had a spiritual awakening as the result of these steps, we tried to carry this message to alcoholics, and to practice these principles in all our affairs.

The Twelve Steps

1. We admitted that we were powerless over our problems and that our lives had become unmanageable.

2. We came to believe that a Power greater than ourselves could restore us to sanity.

3. We made a decision to turn our wills and our lives over to the care of God.

4. We made a searching and fearless moral inventory of ourselves.

5. We admitted to God, to ourselves, and to another human being the exact nature of our wrongs.

6. We were entirely ready to have God remove these defects of character.

7. We humbly asked God to remove our shortcomings.

8. We made a list of all persons we had harmed and became willing to make amends to them all.

9. We made direct amends to such people wherever possible, except when to do so would injure them or others.

10. We continued to take personal inventory, and when we were wrong, promptly admitted it.

11. We sought through prayer and meditation to improve our conscious contact with God, praying only for knowledge of his will for us and the power to carry it out.

12. Having had a spiritual awakening as a result of these steps, we tried to carry this message to others, and to practice these principles in all our affairs.

The Twelve Steps used in *The Life Recovery Workbook* have been adapted with permission from the Twelve Steps of Alcoholics Anonymous.

INTRODUCTION

Once we, too, were foolish and disobedient. We were misled and became slaves to many lusts and pleasures. . . . But— when God our Savior revealed his kindness and love, he saved us, not because of the righteous things we had done, but because of his mercy. (Titus 3:3-5)

This workbook is about transformation from the death grip of an addiction to food to the restoration of life. It's about walking humbly, righteously, and mercifully with God while accepting his will. Often in our addiction, we oppose God, argue with him, plead with him for healing, and methodically cut other people out of our lives. We end up separated from God and from the people that care for us. We feel abandoned by all. The Twelve Steps are a path of finding that humble walk that leads us out of self-centered living that led to eating disorders to acceptance and a closer relationship with God.

We will be examining the Twelve Steps individually to consider the challenging spiritual lessons that allow us to move beyond our compulsions and addictions. Each step has a new task for us in our recovery, but none of the steps stand alone. To effectively move through our bondage to acceptance, we will work the steps in order. Each step prepares us for the next one, as we develop a greater sense of openness to God's plan and purpose in our lives.

The path of recovery involves hard and sometimes painful work. But it is worth the work. We see the Twelve Steps as a path and a process that makes us better disciples and more committed followers of Jesus Christ. Honesty, humility, and courage are vital components of faith that can move us back to a vibrant way of living as a follower of Jesus. Welcome to the journey.

STARTING AND LEADING A GROUP

Recovery is best experienced in the context of a group. Two or more willing people can form a powerful bond as they study and work these steps together. With little effort on your part, your struggles, problems, and hang-ups become a blessing to the group. As you open up, everyone else will feel more free to share from their own lives.

Being the leader of a group is actually quite simple. You can find many books on how to lead a small group, but here's a simple and effective way to do it:

1. Find a location in your home, a church, a workplace, or school, and obtain permission (if necessary) to form the group.
2. Put up a few flyers announcing the time and place, calling it a support group for eating disorders, recovery group, or Twelve Step group.
3. Show up early, arrange the chairs, make some coffee, and welcome people as they arrive.
4. Start when you say you will start by opening in prayer and by reading the Twelve Steps and the correlating Scriptures.
5. Ask if anyone would like to share for three or four minutes. Don't allow others to "fix" the speaker, and if he or she goes on too long, be sure to enforce the time limit.
6. Make sure everyone has a copy of the workbook. Ask them to study Step One for discussion at the next meeting.
7. End when you say you will end by reading the Lord's Prayer.

8. Be sure that everyone knows where to get a workbook and a *Life Recovery Bible*, if they don't already have one.
9. E-mail us—Stephen Arterburn at sarterburn@newlife.com; David Stoop at drstoop@cox.net—and tell us how it's going.
10. Feel good that you are allowing God to use you.

Please remember that working the steps is an art, not a formula. Most often, it is an individualized process.

God be with you on this journey. We pray that you will find healing, serenity, and peace of mind.

PROFILE

When we are overweight or obese, the last thing we want to do is confront the reality of our size. We only look at our face in a mirror, either to put on our makeup, shave, or to fix our hair.

Tammy was like that. She preferred putting on her makeup and fixing her hair in the car, where all she could see in the mirror was her face and her head. Tammy taught third grade and didn't need to look in the mirror to realize her size. While teaching one day, she suddenly noticed that she could no longer fit in the aisles between her students' desks.

When she left school that day, she sat in her car in the parking lot and cried. This experience was a wake-up call. Her overeating was out of control. She knew she was gaining weight but had refused to confront the fact, as many overweight people do. It was time to do something about her weight. Tammy knew she was powerless to control her weight on her own, and her situation had become unmanageable.

The last time she visited the doctor, she had weighed just under 240 pounds. That was two years ago. She decided she had to face the embarrassment of seeing her doctor again and being weighed. When she did, she was told she now weighed 350 pounds. She had heard about Overeaters Anonymous groups, but she had always resisted attending. Now her resistance was done, and she began attending a group regularly.

When she saw the doctor a year later, her weight had dropped to 297 pounds. She marveled at the difference 53 pounds made in her life. It was much easier to walk, work, drive, and even sleep. Looking back to the year before, she was amazed that she had been able to even function as well as she did.

Tammy commented on how her weight was not related to ever being lazy. She was always a hard worker, one that ran around the office doing the work of three in hopes of being accepted by the "normal folks."

For Tammy, weighing 350 pounds was tough. It was hard work carrying all those extra pounds everywhere she went. The good news at this point was that she had given up 53 pounds of baggage—both physically and emotionally—and she is becoming lighter each week. Her goal is to have as little baggage as possible. It takes hard work, dedication, and complete faith in Jesus Christ, but he will carry our load if we will ask him. We are truly powerless to do it in our own strength.

Needless to say, Tammy's emotions have been all over the place. In the past, she always stuffed away the sad, painful emotions by eating large amounts of comfort food. She would eat until she was emotionally numb, which made her feel safe. She has since stopped medicating with food, and it's incredible for her to actually feel her emotions—good and bad. Of course, some days she wants to run to the refrigerator and indulge herself with food. But, amazing as it sounds, this is when she's learning to press into God even harder and ask him to walk with her through the emotions at hand.

STEP ONE

We admitted that we were powerless over our problems and that our lives had become unmanageable.

It's interesting that the first word in the first step is *we*. I can't work on the problems in my life on my own. The resolution comes through the *we*. Tammy increasingly isolated herself over the years from other relationships in order to hide her eating behaviors. Then if her eating suddenly got out of control, no one would be around to see it. She was powerless, but she was not helpless. So she got help. The Twelve Steps teach us that recovery and healing always take place in the context of the *we*.

This is true of anything focused on our spirits. Spiritual transformation always begins in community. At the start of Jesus' ministry, he began by gathering people around him as his disciples. The power of the early church in the book of Acts is directly related to their reputation for loving one another. So even recovery related to our eating disorders needs to take place in some sort of community, whether it's a support group for overeaters, an Eating Disorders Anonymous group, or simply a small group we gather around us. We have to stay connected as we look deep inside ourselves to get an understanding of what creates our insanity.

The key point in Step One has to do with the reality of our powerlessness. It's not a term we like. In fact, it's a term and a reality that we seek to avoid as much as possible. But when it comes to eating issues, we have tried and tried in our own power to overcome the swings in our weight. We lose weight only to gain it back, and we always seem to gain a little bit more on top of what we've lost before.

Admitting that we are powerless is to admit that something or someone has beaten us and is more powerful than our own wills. This injures our pride, so we keep on acting as if we can control food. It's in our sin nature to rebel at the idea of powerlessness because it signifies our inability to escape our life dependencies in our own strength.

To jump into recovery with both feet is good, but we must go even deeper. Not only must we admit and accept our powerlessness over our eating, we must also concede that our lives are unmanageable. This strikes the second blow to our pride and sense of self-sufficiency. When under the influence of addictive thinking, a person believes, "I can handle anything. I can fix this by myself, without anyone else having to be involved."

Here is one example from Scripture of how people can struggle with powerlessness. Naaman had a high-ranking position in the military that blinded him to his powerlessness (see 2 Kings 5:1-15). He began to demand things from life, thinking that he was special because of his position. Like Naaman, we will find that this type of pride that resists input and direction from others is what leads us to isolation. Only God can deal with this rebellion in our hearts. The consequences of our eating disorders are sometimes the only way God can break through to us. For Tammy, it was as simple as not being able to walk down the aisle between the desks in her classroom.

Sometimes we arrive at powerlessness and unmanageability by losing everything, as Job did. Being in recovery and trying to walk a spiritual path does not mean that we will be spared from snags and obstacles. In these times, recovery can appear to be hopeless and not worth the work. The rebel in us that wants control will counsel, "This is just too hard. Your trouble must mean that God doesn't like you." At this point, we need a group of people to continue pointing us to God no matter what happens, people who will nurture hope even in the midst of difficult places. As we hit bottom and face our powerlessness over all of life, we need encouragers.

By exploring our powerlessness, we will have to confront and oppose negative ideas that tell us that being powerless means being a victim. The truth is that by coming to the end of our own power, we develop enough humility to hear the voice of God and do his will.

The apostle Paul—before his conversion and transformation, when he was still known as Saul—could not surrender to his powerlessness because it placed him in opposition to God. He was intoxicated by the power he could wield. Yet God pursued Saul—despite his power-hungry, murderous state of mind—to call him to a new direction, to make him a totally transformed person, and to give him a new purpose. God pursued Saul so that he could stop persecuting the gospel and start preaching it. To accomplish this, God made him totally blind and dependent on others to lead, feed, and shelter him. Saul had to accept his powerlessness in order to be used by God in powerful and amazing ways.

We must first accept our powerlessness and inability to manage before we can be freed from addiction and become a channel for God in ways we could never imagine. We are so schooled in the thought that we can do anything we put our minds to that it is almost impossible to envision the power of God in us doing what we have not been able to do to this point. Shining through human vessels, God is in us and gives us the ability to recover, to accept powerlessness, and to accept inability to manage on our own. We are then open to a life powered by God rather than by our dependencies, our addictions, or our fallible selves.

QUESTIONS FOR **STEP ONE**

Trapped *Genesis 16:1-15*

1. How is my experience of powerlessness similar to Hagar's experience? How is it different?

_____

_____

_____

_____

2. How have I tried to escape from the pain related to my eating issues?

_____

_____

_____

3. What has been my experience of anger in my struggle? What scares me about my anger?

_____

_____

_____

_____

4. How have I experienced sadness related to my eating disorder? What scares me about my sadness?

_____

_____

_____

_____

5. What are some of my fears about facing my issues?

_____

_____

_____

6. Where can I see God in this process right now?

_____

_____

_____

All Is Darkness *Job 6:2-13*

1. Job is very clear about the pain he is feeling. Describe the pain you're experiencing regarding your eating issues.

_____

_____

_____

2. In what ways have I felt totally powerless in my food addiction?

_____

_____

_____

3. In what ways have I tried to be faithful to God in the midst of my compulsive behavior?

_____

_____

_____

4. How can Job's experience help me understand my experience of powerlessness?

_____

_____

_____

Worn Out from Sobbing *Psalm 6:1-10*

1. How does my sadness affect my relationships?

_____

_____

_____

2. In what ways have others misunderstood my food addiction?

_____

_____

_____

3. David seems to project his anger onto God. That's why we need to get comfortable expressing our anger in relationships, especially our relationship with God. Anger can be a protest. In what ways have I brought my protest into a relationship?

_____

_____

_____

4. Who in my circle of friends would be able to help me restore my confidence in God?

_____

_____

_____

Breaking the Cycle *Ecclesiastes 1:1-18*
1. How have I tried to break the cycle of my eating patterns?

_____

_____

_____

2. What strategies have I relied on when I've tried to break the old eating habits?

_____

_____

_____

3. What prevents me from letting go of my own control and declaring that I am powerless?

_____

_____

_____

Like Little Children Mark 10:13-16

1. When I feel powerless, do I feel like a little child? How does that feel?

_____

_____

_____

2. When do I feel most cared for?

_____

_____

_____

3. How does being childlike help me depend on God?

_____

_____

_____

The Paradox of Powerlessness 2 Corinthians 4:7-10

1. Remember some examples of when you have accepted your own powerlessness and embraced God's powerfulness. Describe them in this space below.

_____

_____

_____

2. How do I respond to trouble?

_____

_____

_____

3. How do I respond to being perplexed?

_____

_____

_____

4. What do I do when it feels like God has abandoned me?

_____

_____

_____

_There is great power in our
realizing that we are powerless._

STEP **2**

PROFILE

I (Steve) used to weigh 60 pounds more than I do today. I know the heartache of losing weight, feeling great, and then losing control and gaining it all back. I know how it feels to essentially carry around the equivalent of a third-grader on my person. I know the horror of approaching another summer when everyone will be in a swimsuit and I will have no place to hide.

For years I felt like a second-class citizen because I was fatter than any of my friends. But it was more than that: I was unhealthy. My blood pressure was so high that I was on medication while I was still in my early twenties. I was out of breath and out of energy most of the time. I couldn't run around the block, even at a slow jog! I was facing an early death. And just like you, I had a brain that functioned. My weight problem was not the result of lacking IQ points. The problem went deeper. My problem was emotional and spiritual. Within me there was a stubborn resistance to do what would eventually change my life.

I was counting on my troubled mind—that got me into trouble—to get me out of trouble. I tried the same old tactics over and over, only to fail over and over. Fortunately, I woke up one day feeling sick and tired of being sick and tired. My life was never to be the same again. I had experienced a spiritual awakening that led to a new willingness to change. Based on those changes, I developed the *Lose It for Life* plan—not a diet, but a plan that can work with any diet. Not a behavior plan that leads to a temporary change in the way a person looks, but a healthy plan to address spiritual and emotional needs at the core of a person's being.

It's basically a strategy for a healthy life that I have been living for years, and the results in my own life have been profound. I've seen what poor eating habits can do to a person. Look at my father. His cholesterol was horrible, and he was on blood pressure medication in his early twenties, just as I was. He died at sixty-eight of a massive heart attack. It broke my heart because I had so many plans for us over the years. I realized that I was on the same track for the same health problems as my dad, so I gave up some old family-learned eating patterns and adopted a different life plan. And I still follow it today.

So far so good. I just had an annual checkup, and my blood work was fantastic. Not one indicator was either above or below normal. In the indicators for heart disease, I was one-fourth the risk for heart disease compared to other males my age. I look forward to a long life, and I hope to one day hear that you have experienced the same results.

These radical life changes began from a spiritual place within me—a place of surrender that led me to a new willingness to do whatever it took to get the weight off. I began to lose the weight and have kept it off for over thirty years. That same willingness to learn and heal is the same willingness I try to instill in the hearts of people who attend our workshops. It all began with a willingness to change, and it continues with that same attitude of willingness.

I was forced to face my own powerlessness. I had tried everything to lose weight and everything had stayed the same. What finally worked for me turned into an approach that has helped thousands—the willingness to surrender!

STEP TWO

We came to believe that a Power greater than ourselves could restore us to sanity.

This second step tells us what to do as soon as possible when life throws us a curve. But we typically don't listen because our tendency is to try to deal with the situation on our own terms first. We try to deny the reality of our powerlessness by developing our coping skills. But what this does is multiply our problems instead of solving them. Insanity is sometimes defined as doing the same thing over and over again but expecting different results.

Both Paul and James affirmed this in their letters to early Christians. In his letter to the Romans, Paul says, "We can rejoice, too, when we run into problems and trials" (Romans 5:3). James says, "When troubles of any kind come your way, consider it an opportunity for great joy" (James 1:2). Both Paul and James go on to explain that when our faith is being tested, our endurance in the faith has a chance to grow. Paul adds that "endurance develops strength of character, and character strengthens our confident hope of salvation. And this hope will not lead to disappointment" (Romans 5:4-5).

It takes character to acknowledge that we are powerless and that we need to seek the help of someone who is more powerful than we are. Otherwise we just perpetuate the insanity. In our self-sufficiency, we are under the illusion that God is being unfair or is somehow against us. This was Job's pattern of thinking as he argued with God and protested his innocence. It wasn't until God started asking him questions that he understood how powerless he was and how his protestations only led to a greater degree of insanity.

The Scriptures describe what happens when we try to live in our own power. First, we begin to think that God is unfair, so we begin to question him and wonder if he is really with us, as Job wondered. Our "insanity" in this case is in having the arrogance to think that we could actually see the whole picture as God does and know what is fair or unfair. *Coming to believe* for Job meant accepting that he was a finite human and that God is omniscient and all powerful.

While depending on our own power, we may adopt a grandiose attitude, like King Nebuchadnezzar, and think that we have the right to declare how life should revolve around us, our needs, and our wishes. This king looked at his successes and began to claim the credit for himself. He lost the humility of remembering that God rules and gives power and success "to anyone he chooses" (Daniel 4:32). His grandiosity of thought and attitude was revealed by the dream that he had Daniel interpret. Daniel pleaded with him to turn from his sin of grandiose thinking, and the pride of accomplishment. But Nebuchadnezzar said, "By my own mighty power, I have built this beautiful city as my royal residence to display my majestic splendor" (Daniel 4:30).

Nebuchadnezzar was humbled by God with a season of literal insanity, where he grazed aimlessly with the cattle in the fields. After Nebuchadnezzar's pointless drifting, this king came to his senses by looking up to heaven and realizing that life did not revolve around him, but around God. In the same way, to be relieved of our addictive eating disorders, we realize that our way of dealing with life has not worked. Our years of medicating our emotions with food has not brought the sense of comfort we were seeking. As we face the insanity of choosing to cope with life in these ways, we look up to heaven to find the all-powerful God.

When our hearts and minds are swirling around in the depths of our frustration, we need to find someone more powerful than ourselves to walk the journey with us. Who is more powerful than Jesus? Picture the scene in Matthew 8:23-27. Jesus got into a boat with his disciples and quickly fell asleep in the back. He seemed oblivious to the massive waves in the storm they encountered. Several of his disciples lived on that lake in their work as fishermen. But this was a storm like none that they had ever encountered before. The waves were so big that the disciples, including the fishermen, were terrified. But Jesus continued to sleep.

In their fear and desperation, they woke Jesus with these

words, "'Lord, save us! We're going to drown!' Jesus responded, 'Why are you afraid? You have so little faith!' Then he got up and rebuked the wind and waves, and suddenly there was a great calm" (Matthew 8:25-26). The waves that had been engulfing the boat suddenly stopped, and the sea was still. The wind that had been threatening to sink the boat suddenly stopped. And in that great calm the disciples said in amazement, "Who is this man? . . . Even the winds and waves obey him!" (Matthew 8:27). That's power! And he wants to be our Higher Power, for he is the highest power that exists.

We need the same thing that the woman who suffered from constant bleeding needed. She had tried everything, and nothing had worked. She saw Jesus in the crowd, and thought, "If I can just touch his robe, I will be healed" (Mark 5:28). She is an example of our need to reach out, not just to our brothers and sisters in the Lord, but to the Lord Jesus himself.

Coming to believe in Step Two is a process of our becoming aware of a greater reality than anything we can see with our eyes. God is willing, at any moment, to join with us in our painful emotions. By engaging in this process, we allow God to move us through the process of grappling with our eating disorder and to strengthen our ability to have faith in his power.

QUESTIONS FOR **STEP TWO**

Persistent Seeking *Job 14:1-6*

1. What are my objections to trusting God fully with my eating disorder and with my life?

_____

_____

_____

2. What emotions and questions do I need to be honest with God about?

_____

_____

_____

3. Am I willing to work through the pain and unfairness in my life in order to find God and be freed from the obsessive eating patterns? What holds me back?

_____

_____

_____

Grandiose Thinking *Daniel 4:19-33*

1. How do I display the belief that I am only accountable to myself in my eating patterns?

_____

_____

_____

2. How have I tried to have power over the events, outcomes, and people in my life?

_____

_____

_____

3. In what ways do I show that I have forgotten that God is ultimately in control?

_____

_____

_____

Internal Bondage *Mark 5:1-13*

1. What self-destructive behaviors have I been tempted to do?
   List and describe them.

   _____

   _____

   _____

   _____

2. How have my obsessive eating patterns kept me from living
   in the present? In what ways have I been more comfortable
   living in tombs of isolation and silent judgment?

   _____

   _____

   _____

   _____

3. What motivated me to "come to believe" that I needed to
   rely on Jesus?

   _____

   _____

   _____

   _____

Healing Faith *Luke 8:43-48*

1. How have I tried to control my eating in my own power?
   What were the results?

   _____

   _____

   _____

   _____

2. Am I ready to reach out to Jesus as my Higher Power? Write a note to God about your readiness.

_____

_____

_____

Believe *Romans 1:18-20*

1. What experiences have I had that have shown me that self-sufficiency is not the way I want to live?

_____

_____

_____

2. How have I seen God's power at work in other people's lives? How can those be an encouragement to me as I wait to see God work in my life?

_____

_____

_____

3. What are the signs that I am in the process of being restored to sanity?

_____

_____

_____

Rejoice Always *Romans 5:3-11; James 1:2*

1. How do I think powerlessness relates to my being able to rejoice in the midst of troubles?

_____

_____

_____

2. When I accept my powerlessness and can rejoice in the midst of my pain, what do Paul and James say will be the result?

_____

_____

_____

An Overwhelming Struggle _Romans 8:35-39_

1. Sometimes we feel like giving up the struggle of accepting our own powerlessness. What should I do when those times come?

_____

_____

_____

2. How does it help me in my struggle to realize that God loves me no matter what?

_____

_____

_____

3. What does it mean to me that God cares about even my eating?

_____

_____

_____

Hope in Faith _Hebrews 11:1-10_

1. Am I able to believe that God can help me to live free of my compulsions? How?

_____

_____

_____

2. Can I now believe that as I reach out for God's strength and surrender to him, God's nature is to be present and ready to help? Why or why not?

_____

_____

_____

Faith begins when I believe
that God is who he says he is.

STEP 3

PROFILE

Tammy, whom we met at Step One, has been a great success story. It's been six years since she attended her first New Life workshop, and she is an inspiration to all who attend. She now weighs 140 pounds! She brings her original slacks with her to each workshop to show how she can now fit her entire self into one leg of her old pants.

One of the first lessons she learned was that the issue wasn't about losing weight; it was about developing a whole different attitude toward herself and toward food. She came to the first New Life weekend workshop as a last-ditch effort. She had made up her mind that losing weight was hopeless—she was always going to be obese. But the workshop changed her attitude the very first time she attended. There she learned that it wasn't about weight loss or even keeping the weight off. It was about developing a whole different way of thinking. It was about changing the way she ate. It was about exercise that could be fun. It was about perseverance and staying the course.

She had to see her weight issues in the larger picture of her life and identity. Yes, it was about food, but it was also about keeping her body healthy, which meant that she would have to eat healthy food. Since it was about being with other people in a healthy environment, she determined to get together with several of her friends on a weekly basis to talk about their new approach to life. And it was also about the spiritual issues of her life, issues that she was going to have to take seriously. But it couldn't be about her weight. It had to be about personal transformation.

Tammy started her new program by making sure that her overall health was improving, not simply that she was losing weight. She had to learn how to eat healthfully and some basics about what a healthy diet is. They discussed how to eat a healthy diet at the workshop, and she and her friends continue to learn new things about healthy eating from each other.

Additionally, Tammy had to learn how to manage her emotions rather than being managed by her emotions. She had to take responsibility for her weight problem—she couldn't be the victim anymore. She had to own her previous lifestyle and problems, and she had to learn to distinguish between being physically hungry, being emotionally hungry, and being spiritually hungry.

Tammy had to change her understanding of how God sees her, and she had to change the way she viewed herself spiritually in her relationship with God. She had to experience God's gift of grace and to let go of her judgmental attitude about herself and her body. She had to take the negative thoughts captive and bring them into obedience with Christ (2 Corinthians 10:4-6). In other words, she had to see herself as God saw her: as a part of his beautiful, wonderful creation. But because Tammy was very self-critical and perfectionistic, this was difficult for her to change.

Tammy needed a whole lifestyle change, a personal transformation. But she couldn't have done it by herself. It took God's help and a group of caring friends who were on the same journey as she was. It took time, prayer, study, sharing with friends, and especially perseverance. But the change was worth it for the whole different person she is today.

STEP THREE
We made a decision to turn our wills and our lives over to the care of God.

In Step Three, we decide to surrender our wills, our ways, and in fact, our entire lives over to God. That includes all our losses and all our successes. It sounds like a simple task for us who have turned our lives over to Christ in salvation at some point in time. But this goes beyond salvation. Now we intentionally release our hopes, dreams, choices, relationships, and losses, giving God control over all of it. It is not just a one-time commitment, as we certainly will learn; instead it's meant to be a way of life. This is what Tammy finally understood.

This step calls on—challenges—us to trust God on a deeper level than ever before. Everything we have experienced up to this point may make us somewhat skeptical and wary, especially when we are called upon to trust God completely with our issues. Here we are called upon to give up our self-sufficiency. It's no longer theoretical, it's real. After all, none of the people around us have proven to be trustworthy. Trust has to be repaired and tested. But this of course means we will always struggle to some degree with our ability to trust God, whom we cannot see.

Confronting our lack of trust in God's care is critical in working the rest of the Twelve Steps. For us to move through the process of recovery, we must learn to completely surrender not only *ourselves*, but especially our *wills*. That's the hard part—surrendering our wills. But as Jesus said, "If you give up your life for me, you will find it" (Matthew 10:39).

This is not only a battle of the wills—God's will vs. my will—it's also a spiritual battle. Once again we return to the reality of our powerlessness, where we think we have control but find we really don't. We must face the fact that we live with only an illusion of control. Only God has the ultimate control. Once we accept this, then our dependence on him helps us move through the healing process. For he cares deeply for each of us.

What Step Three maintains, regarding our relationship to recovery, is that we must choose to draw closer to God.

He understands us and our issues. Isaiah describes the future Messiah by saying, "He was despised and rejected—a man of sorrows, acquainted with deepest grief" (Isaiah 53:3). That's why we say God grieves with us. Therefore, he understands our need to grieve as we let go of the past and move into a new future.

In Step One, we admitted that we do not have power over any aspect of our lives. In Step Two, we acknowledged that God has the power to work in our lives. Now in Step Three, we decide to turn everything over to him, let go, and ask for his help. These are acts of humility that allow God's Spirit to draw us close to the Father. When our self-will is out of the way, God can work in our hearts. There may not be immediate results, but in turning it all over to the care of God, we exchange our heavy burdens for the rest and peace that Jesus brings.

As we choose to give our wills, our thoughts, our decisions, our eating habits, and our behaviors "to the care of God," we rest in the belief that he cares for us and he is in control. God is with us no matter what life throws at us. With his power and his presence, we are able to effectively move through this step without being bogged down in despair or hopelessness. Step Three is the foundation of the subsequent actions we will take as we work the remainder of the Twelve Steps.

QUESTIONS FOR **STEP THREE**

Trusting God *Numbers 23:18-24*

1. What in my life has taught me not to trust God?

_____

_____

_____

2. What have I done to cause others not to trust me?

_____

_____

_____

3. What really keeps me from surrendering to God?

_____

_____

_____

It's Your Choice *Deuteronomy 30:15-20*

1. What is it about my understanding of God that blocks me from deciding to turn my life and my will over to his care?

_____

_____

_____

2. How does fear affect my choices?

_____

_____

_____

Doing God's Will *1 Samuel 24:1-11*

1. Can I remember a situation when I knew what God wanted me to do, but I did what I wanted to do? Describe that time here.

_____

_____

_____

2. David had surrendered his will to God's will. What is God's will in reference to my eating disorder? Have I fully surrendered my will to God's?

_____

_____

_____

3. Share an example of when doing God's will was difficult.

_____

_____

_____

Giving Up Control *Psalm 61:1-8*

1. Where did I get the illusion that I can control other people, my circumstances, my job, or my life?

_____

_____

_____

2. What stops me from surrendering my will and my life so that I can find the life God intends for me?

_____

_____

_____

Redeeming the Past *Isaiah 54:4-8*

1. Do I tend to hold God at arm's length? Why?

_____

_____

_____

2. What fears have the most power in my life?

_____

_____

_____

3. How is shame connected to my fears?

_____

_____

_____

Submission and Rest *Matthew 11:27-30*

1. Why do I think I can handle my eating issues on my own with no help from outside myself?

_____

_____

_____

2. How ready am I to learn from others?

_____

_____

_____

3. What aspects of my personality prevent me from learning from and listening to Jesus?

_____

_____

_____

God Is Faithful *Lamentations 3:17-26*

1. What in my circumstances at this point makes it hard for me to believe that God is faithful?

_____

_____

_____

2. Which hopes and dreams of mine have been crushed?

_____

_____

_____

3. As Jeremiah grieves over fallen Jerusalem, he reminds himself of God's faithfulness. What can I call to mind that reminds me of God's faithfulness?

_____

_____

_____

Discovering God *Acts 17:22-28*

1. How would I define the word *surrender*?

_____

_____

_____

2. How would I differentiate between *my will* and *my life*?

_____

_____

_____

There comes a point at which we can either merely have faith, or make a bold move and really live our faith. When we live our faith, we no longer only talk about our beliefs, our lives reflect them: What I believe and say and do all line up. But this alignment only happens when we have enough faith to turn everything over to God—every compartment, every hidden secret, everything—and acknowledge, perhaps for the very first time, that God is the Highest Power in our lives.

4

PROFILE

Andrea was sixteen years old and an only child. Her father was a firefighter, and her mother was a busy stay-at-home mom. Her parents started going to counseling because Andrea's mother was worried sick that her daughter was going to become anorexic. The counselor found that Andrea's mother struggled with extreme anxiety, especially about Andrea. Her father was supportive, but only to a point, because his work as a firefighter kept him very busy.

After a couple of sessions with the parents, the counselor started to meet with Andrea. She confirmed that her mother was extremely anxious, but she also asserted that she didn't need to worry about anorexia. She was just tired of her mother being so controlling. She said her mother forced her to eat everything on her plate, emphasizing the word *forced*.

After meeting several times with Andrea and her parents, the counselor developed a plan for the family. As part of preparing the family to hear the plan, the counselor predicted that they would fail, that the family wouldn't be able to complete the plan. The family responded appropriately by assuring her that they wanted to know what the plan was and that they would faithfully implement it.

The plan was a new ritual. Before every meal, Andrea's mother was to write out a list of what Andrea was supposed to eat at that meal. If her father was present for that meal, he was to be supportive of what her mother asked. Then the mother was to give the list to Andrea, and Andrea could scratch off one of the items— any item she wanted to scratch off. If her father was there, he was to support Andrea's decision. And then when they sat down to eat, Andrea wouldn't have to eat what she scratched off the list.

They were to do this at every meal until they returned for their counseling appointment the next month. They returned one month later, looking a little sheepish. Andrea's mother admitted they had only done this for three of the four weeks, and while it wasn't because they couldn't do it, they were just tired of it. They all agreed to just let Andrea eat whatever she wanted to eat. The fear of anorexia faded into the background.

About ten years later, Andrea made an appointment with the same counselor. She told her counselor that she had been toying with anorexia without knowing what it was called, but that the ritual had changed everything. It had broken the cycle between her and her mother, and she was able to eat normally from that point on. She thanked the counselor. The "eating disorder" was about more than just the eating disorder. It was about control.

STEP FOUR
We made a searching and fearless moral inventory of ourselves.

Up to this point in the Twelve Steps, the work we have done has been related to our thought processes, attitudes, and beliefs. We have moved out of the area of denial into the reality of our addiction to food. We have admitted that we are power-less and have come to believe that only God can and will walk with us through this process. We have surrendered our lives and our wills to the care of God. In other words, we have chosen to let go and let God. Now that this decision has been made, it's time for action.

Our inventory will be a searching and fearless inventory we take of ourselves. This is of immense value in getting to know ourselves. The searching and fearless moral inventory looks back at what our lives have been like up to this point. So get ready. It is often a heartbreaking exercise to face our own brokenness. It is easy to stop the recovery process at this step simply by delaying the start. That's why it's a fearless inventory, for it makes us look at ourselves at a deeper level.

Step Four is designed to answer the question "Who am I?" Early in the history of the Twelve Step program, people began their inventories by looking at how they measured up to the "four absolutes": *honesty, purity, unselfishness,* and *love.* These are positive absolutes, but they are absolutes that everyone at some point fails to meet. So our moral inventories would include our failures to be honest, our failures to be sexually and morally pure, our failures to be unselfish, and our failures to love.

What is an inventory, you ask. Think of how a business takes inventory. They count what supplies and merchandise they have. Taking an inventory tells them what is adequate, what is surplus, what is useless, and what might be a liability.

For example, if we lost a job or we lost our home, we would have to redefine ourselves. We would have to take stock of what life is like now, compare it with what life was like before, and redefine ourselves accordingly. We need to look at our lives spiritually, emotionally, physically, and socially.

The purpose of taking an inventory of our lives is to help us face the truth about ourselves. Truth is the opposite of denial. By putting the truth in writing, we determine that we are ready to break free from the patterns and behaviors of denial. We also know that facing the truth will be painful because we are also facing the reality of what we have lost in our lives. It's never easy to look at our abuses, shame, and disappointments. But even though this is a time of discomfort, we know that the steps of recovery will lead us to humility and to a life full of happiness. It may not feel that way as we work on our inventories, but those who have made the journey before us will testify to that truth.

When Jesus came to earth, he brought with him "grace and

truth" (John 1:14, KJV). Here's how the New Living Translation puts it: "So the Word [Jesus] became human and made his home among us. He was full of unfailing love and faithfulness." This step is a process of facing the truth with God's help. When we face the truth, we also experience God's grace—in his unfailing love. The more we experience the truth, the more we will experience God's faithfulness. And the more we will experience an attitude of humility, have a teachable heart, and feel accepted for who we are.

But we also need to be careful. Our selfish, old sin nature can forget the journey of the first three steps and begin to think very self-centeredly. So we need to approach our inventory with humility, not selfishly. We display our selfishness when we hold on to resentments, are motivated by fear, and are dishonest about our moral or sexual misconduct. All these sins will separate us from God and make it hard for us to know his will and feel his presence as we seek to define what our life is going to be.

The good news about this work is that we will gain an honest picture of ourselves as we face ourselves. Letting go of resentments and fears by working the first three steps has prepared us to define ourselves as authentic followers of Jesus Christ. Serenity and peace of mind will flow into our lives as a result of our surrendering our will and our lives to God.

QUESTIONS FOR STEP FOUR

Coming Out of Hiding Genesis 3:6-13

1. When and how have I led a "double life," trying to look good while full of shame on the inside about my weight and appearance?

_____

_____

_____

2. As I was hiding, in what ways has shame taken root in my heart?

_____

_____

_____

3. Am I ready to deal with "the dirt" so I can live in freedom? What holds me back?

_____

_____

_____

Enter into the Sadness *Nehemiah 8:7-10*

1. What painful memories keep me from going forward in writing my Step Four inventory? Describe them.

_____

_____

_____

2. What am I afraid of facing?

_____

_____

_____

3. What role has shame from past mistakes played in keeping me from starting and completing an inventory?

_____

_____

_____

4. How does pride play into my hiding?

_____

_____

_____

Confession _Nehemiah 9:1-3_

1. What behaviors over my lifetime have been offensive to God?

_____

_____

_____

2. What destructive habits do I need to confess to God?

_____

_____

_____

3. What blocks and resistance do I have to being honest with God?

_____

_____

_____

4. What consequences from past wrong choices am I living with today?

_____

_____

_____

It's All in the Family *Nehemiah 9:14-38*

1. Are there people in my family with whom I need to make things right? Name them here.

_____

_____

_____

2. What unfinished business do I need to face with my family as part of my inventory?

_____

_____

_____

Handling Anger *Matthew 5:21-26*

1. Is my fear of becoming angry holding me back from taking my inventory?

_____

_____

_____

2. The real danger in becoming angry is in venting my anger in unhealthy or harmful ways. Can I be angry and not vent in ways that lead me further from my goal?

_____

_____

_____

3. In the passage in Matthew, Jesus includes making things right so that we can have reconciliation. We will make things right at Step Nine. Will I be able to wait to make

things right? Perhaps include these considerations in your inventory.

_____

_____

_____

Finger-Pointing _Matthew 7:1-5_

1. Is it easier to look at the faults and shortcomings of other people in my life, past and present, than to recognize my own?

_____

_____

2. What is the "log" in my eye, the blind spot that has caused trouble and given rise to pride, finger-pointing, and eventually, my eating disorder?

_____

_____

3. Where and when have I stepped on people's toes and invited retaliation? Have I been proud, blaming, or fearful?

_____

_____

Constructive Sorrow _2 Corinthians 7:8-11_

1. In what ways have I avoided facing my sorrow about how my eating disorder has impacted my life and the lives of others?

_____

_____

2. Have I been willing to set aside time to grieve and to allow humility to grow in me? What stops me?

_____

_____

_____

3. Have I also been self-condemning? What blocks me from experiencing God's grace?

_____

_____

_____

God's Mercy *Revelation 20:1-15*

1. Taking a moral inventory of myself here on earth will help to prepare me for the life to come. How do I still resist making an inventory?

_____

_____

_____

2. As I trusted God in Step Three, am I able to let go of my pride and fear in Step Four and allow his will to be expressed through me? If so, write out a prayer of trust and willingness to complete Step Four.

_____

_____

_____

3. Write down a list and description of fears, resentments, wrongdoings, and character flaws. (Remember that honesty and humility are character strengths that you are building

here, so be as thorough and honest as possible to move toward long-term recovery.)

a) Fears:

_____

b) Resentments:

_____

c) Wrongdoings (actions I have committed that oppose God's standards):

_____

d) Character flaws:

_____

4. After careful self-examination, am I more convinced than ever that I need a Savior every day—not just for salvation, but to walk in freedom from eating disorders and sin? If so, write out a prayer to God that expresses your complete dependence upon him for salvation and freedom.

_____

_____

_____

_____

_____

In Psalm 119:29, the writer pleads with God: "Keep me from lying to myself." Our inventory, when compiled with honesty and diligence, is the beginning of facing the truth about our need to grow in character and maturity, in spite of our losses. It is welcoming the new, authentic me.

PROFILE

Gloria is in her sixties. She's been in Alcoholics Anonymous for several years now because of her husband's alcoholism. She never thought of using the Twelve Steps to deal with her weight issue; she just never made the connection. She would usually follow this pattern: Every now and then she would become so frustrated that she would go to see a nutritionist. He would tell her to take certain supplements and to stay away from sugar. For a few days she would be faithful, and then the craving for something sweet would overtake her, and she would be off her diet.

Gloria formed some bad eating habits in her life. She loved to have a latte in the morning but only if it was sweetened. She loved doughnuts and pastries, especially chocolate. When she would get a latte, she would always be tempted to order a doughnut or a favorite pastry to go along with her drink. She would try to sweeten her latte with a sugar substitute, but it never tasted quite the same as when it was sweetened with real sugar.

She finally went to a counselor to try to understand her behavior, and it was clear to the counselor that she was addicted to sugar. She saw the pattern of getting frustrated with her weight, going to the nutritionist, getting off sweets for a couple days, and then not being able to resist the doughnut, especially the chocolate one. The counselor told her she was an addict—she was addicted to sweets.

The counselor went a step further and suggested she work the Twelve Steps about her addiction to sweets. Having been in Alcoholics Anonymous, it was easy for Gloria to make the transition, but she found that working the steps for your own addiction was quite different than working the steps because you were living with somebody else's addiction. She knew she was powerless to break the cycle. She didn't fight that point. She already knew her Higher Power was supposed to be Jesus, but now she started to slow down in the process. She had prayed about this problem for years, and so far God hadn't helped. Nothing had happened. Turning her addiction over to Jesus felt like the same frustration she had experienced when she prayed about deliverance. So she would relapse, and then start over.

She had quit going to the counselor since she now had another program. But after several relapses where she went on a sweets binge, she went back to the counselor and finally talked through her frustrations. The counselor wisely reminded her that the first step begins with the word *we*. When Gloria finally understood she couldn't do it alone, she brought other people into the process with her as her support system, and now she is winning the battle against her addiction to sweets. She has three months of sobriety!

STEP FIVE

We admitted to God, to ourselves, and to another human being the exact nature of our wrongs.

Doing a fearless moral inventory is not a simple task. It isn't something we can do in a couple minutes. To look deep into ourselves takes time and courage. Some people never get to Step Five because they simply give up and don't even try Step Four. But we were fearless, and we did our inventory. Now we must do something equally difficult: We must confess our wrongdoings. Admitting to God is one thing, but telling another person takes it to a whole different level. If we have to admit everything to someone else, we'll be found out. We'd much rather keep our inventories secret.

This step comes directly from James 5:16: "Confess your sins to each other and pray for each other so that you may be healed." Confession has been practiced throughout the history of the church in many different ways. Today, in many of our Christian communities, confessing to our fellow Christians has fallen out of practice in favor of only confessing to God. We feel too vulnerable and too exposed and too embarrassed when we tell other people what we've done wrong. It's crucial for our salvation that we confess our sins to God. But James makes a very important connection between confessing our sins to one another and our ability to be healed.

Without confession to God and to one another, we cannot experience full healing. Without healing, our addiction and our sins continue to fester. In Jeremiah 6:14, the prophet says, "They offer superficial treatments for my people's mortal wound. They give assurances of peace when there is no peace." Here's how *The Living Bible* paraphrased this verse: "You can't heal a wound by saying it's not there!" There is something important about confessing to another person that plays a key role in our healing.

Step Five uses the word *admitted*, and the Bible uses the word *confess*, but they mean essentially the same thing. When we confess, we admit that we agreed with what happened. We align ourselves with the truth, and we align ourselves with God.

To work Step Five, we must reach another level of humility and willingness. To have God in all parts of our hearts and lives, we must be able to admit our exact wrongs honestly and openly. By sharing our stories of poor choices, poor relationships, and poor reactions to our life circumstances, we get a clearer picture of ourselves. This confessional step initiates a new direction in our lives as we begin to live in a way that seeks to please the Spirit of God and harvests everlasting life.

Who should this person be to whom we will entrust our moral inventory? Who can we trust to be part of our healing process? Jesus is our model for the type of person we should seek. We need someone who is more interested in our spiritual wholeness and our freedom and progress in recovery than in the individual issues we share. Ideally, we can find someone who has been through the Twelve Steps personally and who can listen with compassion and acceptance, not with judgment. When we have completed this step, we may have a mixture of feelings, from relief to gratitude to confusion. We have now inventoried and disclosed our deepest moral and spiritual secrets. We have faced some difficult aspects of ourselves that we have wanted to deny before. Adhering to this process is an additional surrender in itself.

In terms of our fearless moral inventories, if we confess the exact nature of our wrongs to ourselves, to God, and to another human being, God not only forgives everything we confess, but he cleanses us of all the wrong things that we may not even realize we have done. This truth is expressed in 1 John 1:9, which says: "If we confess our sins to him, he is faithful and just to forgive us our sins and to cleanse us from all wickedness." What a great promise for those who confess!

QUESTIONS FOR STEP FIVE

Overcoming Denial *Genesis 38:1-30*

1. What am I avoiding in Step Four by delaying Step Five?

_____

_____

_____

2. What is the exact nature of my wrongs as listed in my fearless moral inventory?

_____

_____

_____

3. Why am I afraid to have someone hear my confession of my inventory?

_____

_____

_____

4. What interferes with my being honest about myself?

_____

_____

_____

Crying Out to God _Psalm 38:9-16_

1. To some people, an eating disorder is a disease. They are afraid of it. Has anyone withdrawn from me because they believed that? How did that make me feel?

_____

_____

_____

2. Have I felt abandoned by friends because of my eating issues? What do I do with my feelings of abandonment?

_____

_____

_____

3. How do I keep focused on God, who always understands the pain of my shame?

_____

_____

_____

Joyful Confession *Isaiah 43:25–44:5*

1. In what ways does my life feel like a parched field?

_____

_____

_____

2. In what ways have I neglected to feed my spirit?

_____

_____

_____

3. In what ways have I experienced God's longing to replenish my life?

_____

_____

_____

4. Have I set the appointment for completing Step Five by sharing my Step Four inventory? My commitment to myself:

Date   Time   Who

_____

_____

_____

Covenant Love *Hosea 11:8-11*

1. How do I react to the truth that God does not give up on me?

_____

_____

_____

2. What keeps me from being truthful with God?

_____

_____

_____

3. What makes me think I can hide anything from God?

_____

_____

_____

The Plumb Line *Amos 7:7-8*

1. Have my morals and values been in line with God's? Explain.

_____

_____

_____

2. Where have I had difficulty applying my morals and values in my life?

_____

_____

_____

3. What has kept me from staying in line with God's morals and values?

_____

_____

_____

4. Am I ready to surrender to God's moral plumb line? If not, why am I hesitating?

_____

_____

_____

Healing through Confession _James 5:16-18_

1. How do I resist confessing my inventory to another person?

_____

_____

_____

2. How do I react to the fact that it isn't enough to confess to God alone?

_____

_____

_____

3. Make a decision: To whom will I read my inventory?

_____

_____

_____

A great weight is lifted when we confess.

PROFILE

Mara Selvini Palazzoli was the director of the Center for
Family Studies in Milan. She tells the story of Lisa, an eight-
year-old girl who had stopped eating.* Her older sister was viva-
cious and outgoing and was very popular with the other kids at
her school. She was ten years old and attended the local public
school. Lisa, on the other hand, attended a private school for
children with special needs, even though there was no appar-
ent reason for her to be there. It was her parents' choice that
she attend that school. The teachers at that school believed she
needed special care, which resulted in her being isolated from
her classmates.

Lisa's basic pattern during the school year was to choose
not to eat a meal periodically. She claimed she didn't feel well
enough to eat. It was interesting that her symptoms disappeared
over the summer. But when she went back to school, her parents feared that unless something changed, she would become
anorexic. The more they tried to get her to eat, the less she ate.

Her father made the call to the counseling center. He told
the counselor that it seemed there was no explanation for what
was going on. She had all the privileges that she needed—
private school, an excellent teacher who took special care of
her, and a caring family. The father didn't want Lisa to come

---

* Mara Selvini Palazzoli, *The Work of Mara Selvini Palazzoli* (Northvale, NJ: Jason
  Aronson, Inc., 1988), 107–120.

to the first counseling session, because he didn't want her to be singled out as being the problem. The counselor understood.

When the parents showed up, the counselor was struck by the differences between Mom and Dad. Dad was a very successful businessman, active socially and an avid sports fan. He seemed like a typical good father who was active in his own life and in the lives of his children. The mother presented herself very modestly, devoted to her husband and to her family at home. She seemed overly submissive and overly passive. The older sister seemed to be a carbon copy of the father, and Lisa was a carbon copy of her mother. Only it went further with Lisa, for the parents felt there was something wrong with the way Lisa was.

When the counselor met with the two sisters alone—without the parents—she noted that Lisa didn't act at all like the way the parents described her. The sisters behaved together in a way that was like any other two sisters who cared for each other might act. Lisa was the opposite when the sisters met with the parents.

As the counseling continued, the counselor felt that Lisa did not have special needs and did not need to attend a special school. The parents listened to the counselor. Although it took some time for them to agree with the counselor, they eventually pulled Lisa out of the special school and put her in the same school that her sister attended.

Her anorexic symptoms disappeared almost overnight. Sometimes eating is the one thing under our control, and this is especially true for children. When a child stops eating, unless there is a medical reason for it, find out why they have "gone on strike." Lisa was protesting having to go to a different school, and finally someone listened.

STEP SIX

We were entirely ready to have God remove these defects of character.

Step Six is a pause in the process of the Twelve Steps. There is nothing that we do and no action is required in this step. It's for getting ready. Before we can experience behavioral changes in our lives, we first need to experience a change in our hearts. In Hebrew, the language of the Old Testament, the word often translated as *heart* means "the center of our being." That's why we can say our healing comes from the heart, the center of who we are.

Our willingness to change is the point of this step, just as it was the point of Jesus' encounter with the man at the pool of Bethesda, as described in John 5. The man Jesus talks to has been at that pool for thirty-eight years. It was his home. It was where his friends were. It was the center of his life. So it was a serious question when Jesus asked him, "Would you like to get well?" (John 5:6). If he didn't have to sit at the pool every day, what was he going to do with all his time? Jesus was asking if the man was willing to have his whole life changed.

The man never directly answers Jesus' question. Instead, he makes a valid observation. He says he has no one to get him to the water in time to be healed. That may suggest a willingness to change. The man was truly powerless and apparently willing, and so Jesus did for him what the man couldn't do for himself.

This step simply questions our willingness. There's nothing else we need to do for this step. In fact, it asks us, "Are you entirely ready?" The previous two steps examined what needs to be changed in our lives. Here we have a step that merely asks if we're ready to change. Why this step? Because the focus is different. It's not asking if we are going to change, as if we're going to do it ourselves. We know that doesn't work because we've tried it in the past. Step Six is asking us if we are ready to do it right this time—to let God do the changing.

Why would we not be ready? Some of our character defects have been useful to us and have sometimes been necessary for survival. It can be very difficult to let them go when they are so automatic and so deeply ingrained in us. This process of becoming "entirely ready" can bring grief. Not only are we grieving our loss of control, we might also be letting go of old friends and our old ways of life. There's a part of us that says we don't want to move forward because that means we have to let go of the past—we have to let go of our old way of life. But the past is supposed to be a process, not a persistent way of life.

Our inventory was only the first half of the process through which, when we complete it, we'll be on our way to character building. Now we must begin to allow God's Spirit to work deep in our hearts, rooting out our defects of character and making changes in our behavior and attitude that will bring wholesomeness and serenity.

So we need to see that this isn't an all-or-nothing step, even though it may feel that way. Remember it's a step about *willingness*. Are you willing to change? It's like what the apostle Paul said about his personal journey: "I don't mean to say that I have already achieved these things or that I have already reached perfection. But I press on to possess that perfection for which Christ Jesus first possessed me" (Philippians 3:12). Paul's reference to perfection is not what we think of when we think of perfection. Paul is simply talking about his progress toward the goal of excellence—being everything God wants him to be.

That's the way it is with Step Six. It's like we're on the edge of a new phase in our lives. Up to this point, we have been wrestling with the decision to surrender our character defects and our previous ways of life. Our attitude is the main thing. This is the step where we are asked to take ownership of our character defects and our losses. It's wishful thinking that God will just take them away. When we are willing to give them up, we become a part of a special process. It's a simple formula: "Sin is the problem, Jesus is the cure, and the result is a miracle."

The key to this step is for us to have a "broken and repentant heart" (Psalm 51:17). When King David finally faced himself, he realized that nothing had given him the key to success in God's eyes—not his pride, his position in life, or his previous achievements. It was only through his brokenness that he was able to experience success in living according to God's standard. God loves us with faithful love, but his love for us is more fully experienced when we come to him in an attitude of humility, of brokenness. The early developers of the Twelve Steps called this step the "Step of Repentance." Repentance means turning around and going in a different direction. That's what Step Six calls for!

QUESTIONS FOR **STEP SIX**

Time to Grieve *Genesis 23:1-4; 35:19-21*

1. What is standing in the way of me being able to change the way I eat? Make a list of your reasons. Be specific.

_____

_____

_____

2. What defects of character are standing in my way of changing?

_____

_____

_____

Healing Our Brokenness *Psalm 51:16-19*

1. Have the last five steps prepared me to be "entirely ready" for God to work in my heart and my life?

_____

_____

_____

2. In this psalm, David had to grow up a little. He had to accept that he was flawed in God's eyes. He could never bring a sacrifice good or perfect enough to atone for those flaws. Am I still trying to bring God evidence of how good I am, or am I coming to a place of acceptance, as David did? How does acceptance help me to stay in the healing process? Explain:

_____

_____

_____

3. Jesus said, "God blesses those who mourn, for they will be comforted" (Matthew 5:4). In what ways has God comforted me?

_____

_____

_____

God's Abundant Pardon *Isaiah 55:1-9*

1. What ways have I tried to fill the hunger of my soul and the thirst of my spirit with activity, instead of trusting in God and following his will?

_____

_____

_____

2. Do I believe, not just in my head but in my heart, that the life God has for me in the future will be even more satisfying than the one I've lived up to this point? Is my heart willing?

_____

_____

_____

Going Deeper *Jonah 4:4-8*

1. What deeper problems have I uncovered in myself?

\
\
\

2. What difficulties have I suffered that have revealed deeper hurts?

\
\
\

3. Am I willing to have these defects removed by God? Why or why not?

\
\
\

Discovering Hope *John 5:1-15*

When we are ready, God does his part. Our part is to get rid of our excuses, our stubborn resistance, and our fear of change. When we clear out these blocks and become entirely ready, it becomes clear that God must do the rest, because only he can accomplish the miracle of setting our feet on the path of an authentic life again.

1. What are my excuses for not moving forward in my recovery?

\
\
\

2. Have I been stubbornly resistant because I've been afraid of change? Why am I afraid of change?

Attitudes and Actions *Philippians 3:12-14*

This is the attitude of Step Six: "Work hard to show the results of your salvation, obeying God with deep reverence and fear. For God is working in you, giving you the desire and the power to do what pleases him" (Philippians 2:12-13).

1. Do I have a vision for the purposes for which God has saved me spiritually? Describe those purposes here.

---

2. Am I now willing to accept that I will continue taking this step in order to grow, letting go of the old way of life to make room for my new life? Why or why not?

Removing Impatience *James 1:1-4*

1. I am to rejoice, not in the troubles that come my way but in the opportunities that troubles present for me to grow. What is my typical attitude toward troubles?

---

2. How does knowing that my troubles give me the opportunity to grow affect my attitude about my experience of my troubles?

_____

_____

_____

3. How can I develop more patience when troubles come my way?

_____

_____

_____

*First Peter 4:1 tells us to arm ourselves
with the attitude of Christ, who was prepared
and willing to suffer. It's time to get ready.*

STEP **7**

PROFILE

Over the years, Glenn's weight had gradually ballooned to 260 pounds. He was tall, so it didn't look too bad, but he knew the price he would pay if he kept that weight on. When he graduated from high school thirty-five years ago, he weighed 210 pounds, which he considered to be his ideal weight. It only took his moving up a couple of pounds for him to realize that something about his eating patterns had to change.

Glenn was determined not to follow a special diet because it had never worked for him in the past. He had lost some weight, but like with everyone else, he had gained it all back— along with a few extra pounds. This time he was determined to change the way he ate and the way he would eat for the rest of his life. The old destructive behaviors had to go.

He determined he was going to break it down into two "sets" of weight loss. He would follow the first set until he reached a loss of 20 pounds. He set no time limit, only that he would continue to gradually lose weight. When he reached his goal, he would take six months off from losing weight, and learn to eat in order to maintain his weight at 240 pounds. Six months later he had reached his first goal.

He accomplished his first goal by cutting down the volume of his eating. For example, instead of a whole hamburger for lunch, he would eat half, skip the fries, order a big glass of water, and throw the other half of the hamburger away. He would eat a good breakfast and then have a very light dinner.

The first week was difficult because he struggled with feeling hungry a lot. He knew that his stomach was adjusting and that it would eventually accept half of a lunch as filling. What surprised him, though, was learning that he was a comfort-food eater. He enjoyed eating, and he found it to be comforting if he could eat what he wanted regardless of the consequences. So to change his eating pattern, he had to change his motivation from eating for comfort to eating as a part of being alive. He enjoyed his wife's cooking, and she was on board with understanding the changes that he was making.

When he was still at 239 pounds six months later, he decided it was time for his second weight loss "set." Now his goal was to reach 220. He made a few adjustments to his maintenance diet and slowly began moving toward the 220 mark. Five months later, when he hit his goal, he continued on past 220 pounds and ended up at 215 pounds. Again, he went on a maintenance diet. Two years later, he continues to eat that way, and his weight fluctuates between 215 and 218 pounds. He had to buy new clothes, and both he and his wife were delighted with the task.

Not everyone can lose weight this way, but it worked for Glenn. He learned two broad lessons. First, lose weight slowly but consistently. You probably accumulated the excess weight slowly, and you will get rid of it slowly. Second, pay as much attention to maintaining the weight loss as you did to losing the weight.

STEP SEVEN
We humbly asked God to remove our shortcomings.

Step Seven proves the wisdom of working the steps in order from the beginning. Some people just want to jump in anywhere that strikes their fancy. When they do that, their recovery is really neither a process nor a path. This is especially true for Step Seven, which is the culmination of Steps Four through Six. Our pathway began with the readiness and willingness to have our defects removed by God. Before we could be ready and willing, we had to do the Step Four inventory, and then we admitted the truth to ourselves, to God, and to another person. These steps brought clarity to our lives and became the foundation for the rest of our journey. Now our willingness becomes a request that God remove our defects.

That makes this step one of the easiest to do, and yet the hardest. We are asking God to do the work. This will mark a turning point in our recovery. Now we begin to allow God's Spirit to flow into our lives and replace character defects with character strengths. We get out of our own way and literally give control to God.

It's important to understand that God isn't going to fix us instantly, especially with food addiction. It will take time. The truth is that God has a very different plan. His plan will involve other people, tough experiences, and hard decisions. He knows what it takes to change people with potential into people who grow, relate, and make changes the way God wants them to.

The problem with instant change is that it never brings instant character, nor does it help us mature. That's what recovery is all about. It's about our maturing and developing character. It does take time, and God knows that. The other point that's important to make at this juncture is that God doesn't deal with everybody the same way. And if we want to control how God is going to work in us, we have forgotten the early lesson that we are powerless without him and that we turned our wills and our lives over to him.

God's plan is often the work of *opposites*. He challenges us to rely upon him and to ask the Holy Spirit for the power to do the opposite from what we are accustomed to doing. We may argue with our impulses, but then we humbly ask God to give us the strength to move in the opposite direction. We may not have thought well of groups in which people share the intimate details of their lives. Now we have to stop ridiculing those people and do the opposite—to become one of them. Our goal becomes doing the opposite of what we would do when left to our own devices—over and over again.

This step includes the word *humbly*. Our first taste of humility was when we admitted our powerlessness. Now we see that this is just the beginning of a lifelong process in which God brings us closer to his purpose and desire for us. In terms of our eating, humility is also a factor. A big part of our recovery is realizing how powerless we are. It takes humility to allow God to be God, not to simply be our adversary. Remember, God's questioning of Job was to increase Job's humility and to let God be God. And in our recovery, we are learning new things about ourselves as well. Know this: God is always up to something good. For as Paul says, "we can be so sure that every detail in our lives of love for God is worked into something good" (Romans 8:28, MSG).

QUESTIONS FOR **STEP SEVEN**

God My Helper *Exodus 2:1-12*

1. Does the thought of facing life without an eating disorder frighten me? In what ways?

_____

_____

_____

2. Like Moses, do I make excuses as a way to resist change?

_____

_____

_____

3. How is that part of my unwillingness to let God change me?

_____

_____

_____

Clearing the Mess _Isaiah 57:12-19_

1. Have I developed enough humility from my experiences to see that I need to let God work in my heart? Is there any doubt that self-reliance has kept God out?

_____

_____

_____

2. Describe the difference between humiliation and humility.

_____

_____

_____

Giving Up Control _Jeremiah 18:1-6_

1. Have I ever demanded that God have circumstances changed for my benefit? When?

_____

_____

_____

2. Have I ever been impatient about God's timing?

_____

_____

_____

3. What keeps me from letting go so that God can change my life?

_____

_____

_____

_____

4. In my food addiction, have I become impatient with God?

_____

_____

_____

Pride Born of Hurt *Luke 11:5-13*

1. Is it hard for me to ask anyone, even God, for help? If so, why?

_____

_____

_____

2. How has that affected my eating issues?

_____

_____

_____

3. What experiences in my family brought about my self-sufficiency?

_____

_____

_____

4. Do I trust God to meet my needs and to walk with me through my addiction? Why or why not?

_____

_____

_____

A Humble Heart *Luke 18:10-14*

1. Have I ever compared my faults, problems, losses, and sins to blatant sins of others in order to avoid deeper work on my own character defects? What does this do for me?

_____

_____

_____

_____

2. While dealing with my eating issues, have I struggled at all with self-hatred or self-harm? What do I need to do in order to be open with a trusted adviser or counselor about this?

_____

_____

_____

_____

3. Am I humble enough to let others know that I'm facing my food addiction?

_____

_____

_____

_____

An Open Book *Philippians 2:5-9*

1. How important is my image to me?

_____

_____

_____

2. Can I release my self-centered fears of being known and of losing my image? Write a prayer to God expressing the desire to do so.

_____

_____

_____

Unending Love *1 John 5:1-15*

1. What blocks me from asking God to do the work of character building and maturity in my heart and life? Describe each block.

_____

_____

_____

2. How confident am I in believing that God is willing to remove my shortcomings? Describe those feelings.

_____

_____

_____

Shortcomings is a very polite way of describing sin, weakness, defects in character, addiction, compulsions, dependency—or a thousand other conditions and symptoms that indicate we are falling short of the glory of God and the lives he has called us to live. Asking God to remove our short-comings is always a joint venture between us and him. Since we have spent much of our lives proving we can't fix ourselves, it is time to finally ask God to do what we will never have the power or insight to do ourselves.

A Prayer for Step Seven

Dear God,
Search my heart and reveal to me any arrogance or pride that is separating me from you, the people around me, and the person you have called me to be. My shortcomings are numerous, and my attempts to fix them always end in failure. Please remove these shortcomings from me. Do for me what I cannot do for myself. Give me the courage to do whatever it takes to become victorious over these problems. Thank you for the work you are doing in me and for the opportunity to transform my life. Amen.

STEP **8**

PROFILE

Claudia was twenty-two when she decided to see a counselor. She decided to go because one of her friends had warned
her about throwing up after eating. She said it could cause esoph-
ageal cancer. Claudia was scared because she'd been throwing
up regularly since the age of fourteen. That meant she had been
throwing up regularly for over eight years. She decided she could
talk to a counselor about it before checking with her medical
doctor.

Claudia told the counselor she started purging because she
liked to eat, especially some of the things that her mother made.
She admitted that she had a tendency to binge eat, and she
had discovered that she could control her weight by throwing
up after binge eating. If dinner included something she really
enjoyed, she would eat a lot of it. Then while the dishes were
being done, she would sneak to the upstairs bathroom and throw
up. As far as she could tell, her mother never suspected what she
was doing, and her father was oblivious to it.

The counselor was careful with Claudia, knowing that
someone with issues related to bulimia would be fragile.
She approached the underlying issues gently. After gaining
Claudia's trust, one session, she asked Claudia if she enjoyed
eating. Claudia answered, "Hello? Yes! It's one of my life's
joys." Then, after talking about her enjoyment of eating, the
counselor asked, "What happens after you eat something you

really enjoy?" It took some time for Claudia to answer that question. When she did, she said, "I don't really know, but somehow I feel I've got to get rid of what I eat when I enjoy it. Somehow it had to become bad—if left alone it might increase my weight, and that would be bad."

Claudia didn't have much insight into what she had said, but the counselor was pleased with what she did say. She understood that something started out good, but that when it was enjoyed, it would somehow turn bad. Because it was bad, it had to be eliminated. At first Claudia didn't fully understand. She was stuck on either something being good or something being bad. How could it change?

Now the counselor had something more to work on than just the eating issues. The underlying issue was that Claudia was stuck on splitting good and bad—either it was one or the other. Those with anorexia often struggle with a sense that the body itself is bad, but those with bulimia struggle with the belief that in some way, the act of eating turns good food into something bad.

STEP EIGHT

We made a list of all persons we had harmed and became willing to make amends to them all.

Our first reaction when reading this step might be: "It's in the past; it's over and done with. Nothing can be done about it now." But it's often not over. If we don't deal with our past issues, then they can easily be reawakened by events in our present. Step Eight is the only way to deal with our issues in the present and leave them in the past. When that is done, we become open to looking outside of ourselves and moving into healed and restored relationships. It all begins with a list.

Lists are valuable parts of the Twelve Steps. In Step Four, we listed all of the shortcomings and defects we knew about ourselves. Now we need to make a list of people who have been affected by those shortcomings and defects. This will be a list of people we know we have harmed. More than anything, it is a list of relationships that may be healed and restored when we honestly seek to make amends for what we have said and done to hurt others.

Some people's names will be on our list because what we have done against them is so large that it cannot be ignored. There will also be people on the list who might not be as obvious—those who have felt rejected or abandoned by us. No matter how big or how small the offense, we must record the names of those who most likely do not think fondly of us or of their time with us.

This step is a tough way of carrying out Luke 6:31: "Do to others as you would like them to do to you." Wouldn't we all love to get a call or letter from someone who hurt us and hear him or her express regret and remorse? Wouldn't we love to know that, in the end, this person was not gloating over what was done to us but instead wanted to make it right? Such restitution has rarely happened in our lives because so few people can humble themselves enough to admit they were wrong, let alone be willing to make amends to those who paid the price for their actions.

Once our lists are complete, we must once again exercise our will. Each entry may come with a host of excuses for why we should not make amends. But take note that this step concludes with a very significant word: *all*. Our willingness to make amends must encompass every entry on our lists, even if later we might discover some valid reasons that it wouldn't be wise or helpful to make amends to everyone we have harmed.

This step is only for making the list and for becoming willing to make amends. Once we have made the list as complete as possible at this time, that's all we have to do for this step. The decision about whether to make amends with someone is part of the next step.

Willingness is a huge aspect of all facets of recovery. We cannot work on any of the steps without being willing. And we cannot work any of the steps well unless and until we have come to the place where we are willing to do whatever it takes to recover or work though our eating issues.

A big part of our recovery has to do with a willingness to move forward in the process with someone. This can be a problem for couples, for often husbands and wives approach making amends differently. Because of this, often our recovery partner for this step will be a good friend or a sensitive relative.

One thing to watch out for at this step is rationalization. We can rationalize a lot of people off our lists by focusing on what they did to us or thinking of our horrible act as a merely crummy act. But the key is to focus on your own behavior in relation to that person. Another caution has to do with defensiveness. It is easy to obsess about the fact that they should be contacting us and to decide that the other person should be the one to make the first move. We have to get beyond our naturally defensive thoughts and focus on our own responsibility.

One more thing: Often when we make a list of people we have hurt, we leave off the person who has experienced more pain than anyone else—*ourselves*. You must acknowledge that you have hurt yourself, and you must put your name at the top of the list of people you have harmed. Willingness to forgive ourselves and make amends to ourselves makes it easier to do the same for others.

QUESTIONS FOR **STEP EIGHT**

Making Restitution *Exodus 22:10-15*

1. How have I failed to respect the property of others?

_____

_____

_____

2. How have I avoided responsibility?

_____

_____

_____

3. What excuses have I used for not looking at my own behaviors?

_____

_____

_____

Unintentional Sins *Leviticus 4:1-28*

1. In what ways have I unintentionally harmed others with my words, moods, self-pity, depression, anger, or fears?

_____

_____

_____

2. In what ways have I acted thoughtlessly and without regard for others' needs or feelings?

_____

_____

_____

Scapegoats *Leviticus 16:20-22*

1. Have I been putting off making a list because I am afraid of some responses? Who am I afraid of? Why?

_____

_____

_____

2. Is there someone I'm having trouble forgiving who blocks my
   willingness to work through this step? Who?

   _____

   _____

   _____

Coming Out of Isolation *Ecclesiastes 4:9-12*

1. How have I allowed isolation to block or slow down my facing
   my addiction?

   _____

   _____

   _____

2. What is the role of shame and guilt in my isolation?

   _____

   _____

   _____

3. Am I willing to forgive myself for the hurt I've caused others?
   How about forgiving myself for the hurt I have caused
   myself? Write a prayer of willingness to forgive.

   _____

   _____

   _____

   _____

   _____

   _____

   _____

Forgiving Others, Forgiving Yourself *Matthew 18:23-35*

1. Are there people on my list who I am having trouble forgiving for their part in our relationship? Who and why?

_____

_____

_____

2. What stops me from letting others off the hook? Fear? Resentment? Care taking?

_____

_____

_____

3. What blocks me from forgiving others for the wrongs they have done to me?

   a. Fear of what others would think of me?
   b. Fear of letting others see my hurts?
   c. Fear of conflict?
   d. Protecting others' feelings to avoid conflict?

_____

_____

_____

Grace-Filled Living *2 Corinthians 2:5-8*

1. Is there anyone, either on my list or not, whose behaviors I do not approve? Who? Why?

_____

_____

_____

2. Am I willing to let go of judgment and disapproval to open myself to the recovery process and to working this step?

_____

_____

_____

3. Have I been so afraid of rejection that I have delayed my recovery process? What about my willingness to make amends?

_____

_____

_____

The Power of Words *James 3:5-10*

1. Words can hurt terribly. Who has been hurt by my misuse of words?

_____

_____

_____

2. James calls the tongue a "flame of fire." How have I tamed my tongue?

_____

_____

_____

3. What have been the consequences of my misuse of words?

_____

_____

_____

Remember, it's about willingness!

STEP **9**

PROFILE

Alex suffers from binge eating. His disorder differentiates itself from bulimia in that he doesn't have to throw up. Sometimes he does throw up, but it's more out of discomfort. He overeats compulsively. Presently he is obese, weighing over 280 pounds. A binge eater is someone who continues eating until well past feeling satisfied. He also eats quickly and keeps on eating when a normal person would stop. He will eat compulsively when he isn't even hungry.

Alex is embarrassed by how much he eats, but that's not enough to change his behavior. His eating is a compulsive act that is beyond his control. So to avoid embarrassment, he mostly eats alone. When he is with his family, he will join them for meals, even though it means he will be embarrassed by some of his behavior.

When he eats with his family, he wishes he could overcome his tendency to ask if he can have any leftover food from other people's plates. Before they sit down to eat, he's determined not to do that, but he can't help himself. It's just part of the addiction.

When a friend suggested that he join a Twelve Step group, he decided to check it out. It has been like a breath of fresh air. He easily understood the fact that he was powerless, because he knew well how powerless he was. He also knew that his life was unmanageable and that he was living in a form of insanity.

He didn't resist when the person who recommended he do the Twelve Steps suggested that his Higher Power be Jesus. He was happy to do that, just like he was happy to turn his will and his life over to the care of God. He was desperate, and it all made sense to him.

When he got to Step Four, it got difficult. But with the help of his friend who was like his sponsor, Alex tackled doing the fearless moral inventory. It took him some time, but he had lots of time. He made a thorough inventory, read it to God, read it to his friend, and reread it himself. It's been two years since he began Twelve Step recovery, and his bouts with binge eating have diminished to only once or twice a month. He's on the road to recovery, and he will share his story with anyone who will listen.

STEP NINE

We made direct amends to such people wherever possible, except when to do so would injure them or others.

You may notice that in Step Nine, we put into practice the principles of the previous eight steps: powerlessness, restoration to sanity, willingness, and seeking help. Now we add the important principle of making amends.

The word *amend* means "to put right or to change." That means we are not talking about a simple apology but a serious change of attitude on our part where we also admit to causing pain and loss in another person. Unless we confess our wrongs to at least one other person, we will find our healing incomplete. If we can talk, write, phone, text, or e-mail the person we have harmed, we need to do so. If the person is not alive, or cannot be located or contacted, we need to at least confess to another person to get the secret out. Finally, if we cannot make amends directly to the person we harmed, perhaps we can make amends in another way.

In Genesis 32–33, we see this step in action. Jacob had to flee his home because he feared that his brother was going to kill him. He stayed away for many years. Then God directed him to go home. On his way home, Jacob reached out to his brother in peace because he hoped that Esau would be friendly (Genesis 32:5). Clearly, Jacob was still afraid that Esau would kill him. When Esau responded to Jacob's message by meeting him with an army of 400 men, Jacob was afraid (Genesis 32:6-7). Jacob had no idea whether his brother intended to kill him or if he had put Jacob's offenses out of his mind.

So Jacob determined to make amends to his brother Esau by sending ahead of his group a gift of herds of various livestock (Genesis 32:13-16). To Jacob's surprise, after he bowed to the ground seven times, Esau ran to meet him and embraced him (Genesis 33:3-4). Esau asked Jacob, "'What were all the flocks and herds I met as I came?' . . . Jacob replied, 'They are a gift, my lord, to ensure your friendship'" (Genesis 33:8-9). Even though Esau wasn't planning to kill him anymore, Jacob still made amends to Esau.

We don't know what Esau's intentions were when he brought 400 men with him to meet his brother, Jacob. And Esau had no idea what Jacob's intentions were when he came home. But Jacob knew he had harmed his brother—which is why he had to leave home in the first place—and he was ready to make amends regardless of his brother's intentions.

This step also includes a qualifier to making amends—*except when to do so would injure them or others*. That can be wrongly used as an excuse not to make amends, rather than as a protection for those who have been hurt. It can allow us to walk away from life-changing opportunities, for ourselves and for others.

If the people we have sinned against are too weak or sensitive or wounded, and they may be hurt further by our confession, then perhaps this is not the right time to confess. Nevertheless, we can begin to work toward making amends when it is the right time. And when the time comes, we do not necessarily have to tell the truth one-on-one or alone. We may need the help of a counselor to make the process go as well as possible. We may also need the counselor's help in teaching us the language of forgiveness. The resolution may not be quick, but we should strive to make it happen at the most effective time possible.

This is a very tough step, but in some ways it makes more sense than any other step. At least the purpose is easier to understand. Quite simply, it is not enough in every case for us to apologize for what we have taken from others without offering to make restitution. It might be enough if they accept the amends but do not want further contact. It might be enough just to say we're sorry, if there is no tangible way to make it right. But more often than not, there is a way to make amends that includes complete restoration, especially if two people can work through their differences and resolve the damage and the pain to make things right.

In Matthew 5:23-24, Jesus clearly shows how important this step is to God: "So if you are presenting a sacrifice at the altar in the Temple and you suddenly remember that someone has something against you, leave your sacrifice there at the altar. Go and be reconciled to that person. Then come and offer your sacrifice to God." Here is the God of the universe, who deserves and demands our worship, telling us that there is something he desires even more than our worship—a clean slate in our relationships.

The amends process and Steps Eight and Nine bring out the "unfinished business" in our lives. We may discover past traumas that must be faced and dealt with if we are to maintain our recovery. It is important not to do this alone but to talk with your counselor or another trusted adviser about what these steps bring to the surface. We may not have caused or asked for these traumas to occur, but we may have to make amends to ourselves for playing the victim or curtailing our lives as a result of trauma.

Restoration of relationship with ourselves is an important outcome of Step Nine. There is no more need to run when we have gone face-to-face with those we have harmed and sought to make things right. There is no longer any need to run because the slate is clean. We no longer need to speculate about forgiveness—we have forgiven, and we have received forgiveness.

QUESTIONS FOR STEP NINE

A Feared Encounter Genesis 33:1-11

1. Who are the people on my Step Eight list who strike the most intense fear in my heart when I think about making amends face-to-face?

_____

_____

_____

2. Do I have support people who will remind me again of my willingness to take such a challenging step?

_____

_____

_____

Keeping Promises 2 Samuel 9:1-9

1. How has my food addiction made me aware of people with whom I need to make amends?

_____

_____

_____

2. Is there anyone to whom I owe amends due to forgetting to fulfill a promise?

_____

_____

_____

Hope for Those Making Amends _Ezekiel 33:10-16_

1. What type of amends listed in Step Eight do I resist? Why?

_____

_____

_____

2. What are the fears that are keeping me from the life-giving process of Step Nine?

_____

_____

_____

Peacemaking _Matthew 5:23-26_

1. Am I a peacekeeper or peacemaker?

_____

_____

_____

2. What is my usual response or reaction to brokenness?

_____

_____

_____

3. Does my amends list include people who have something against me? Does that make it hard for me to have the courage to deal with them?

_____

_____

_____

The Blessing of Giving _Luke 19:1-10_

1. List the financial amends that you owe. Name the people and amounts:

_____

_____

_____

2. Am I willing to go to any lengths to offer amends, even when it calls for payments to be made?

_____

_____

_____

A Clean Slate _Ephesians 2:8-10_

1. How does knowing my heart is clean before God help me make amends with people?

_____

_____

_____

2. What did I learn from the passage about my clean heart?

_____

_____

_____

3. What does my making amends say about my character?

_____

_____

_____

Unfinished Business _Philemon 1:13-16_

1. Have any relationships or past wrongs come to light in the process of recovery where I still need to make amends?

_____

_____

_____

2. Do I have any unfinished business left on my list?

_____

_____

_____

3. Am I waiting for the certainty of forgiveness before I make amends? Why am I afraid of a lack of certainty?

_____

_____

_____

The Servant's Heart _1 Peter 2:18-25_

1. Am I being reluctant to make amends while I am dealing with my eating issues?

_____

_____

_____

2. Do I fear that painful consequences will cause me more suffering? If so, what is the worst that could happen?

_____

_____

_____

3. Which of the previous steps do I need to focus on before making these fearsome amends?

_____

_____

_____

4. Do I trust God's will for me if I follow the challenge of Step Nine?

_____

_____

_____

There is a price to be paid for freedom,
and it is called restitution.

PROFILE

John found it was possible to lose weight and keep it off. He had lost 90 pounds—his goal—and he had been keeping his weight steady for almost a year. His journey required him to make necessary changes that were not easy. He also found he had to stay on his toes in order to stay the course. But then, John relapsed. He reverted to his old unhealthy eating patterns.

He had forgotten to recognize the signs of possible relapse that occur early, so he did not know he was in dangerous waters. Before John got back on track, he had regained 8 pounds. As he worked to lose those 8 pounds—which wasn't easy—he determined that relapse was going to be a thing of the past for him. He was going to relearn all the things that he had forgotten about relapse and make any necessary changes to protect himself from that possibility.

The first thing you remember is that a relapse is more than a slip. It is more than just a return to overeating. For John, it was a return to all the old patterns of life that included overeating. Relapse is always preceded by a process which generally involves a predictable progression that gradually moves you farther and farther away from doing what you know worked in the first place. It's then that you lose control.

For John, he recognized that he had started to focus on his fear of failing. Along with that fear, he had even started feeling sorry for himself that he had to be so consciously aware of what he was going to eat. This had led him to feel like he was the victim and that life was unfair. Why should he have to struggle with how he ate? He became very self-critical and negative about himself and everyone in his life. His wife reminded him that at work, he had grown more and more irritated with his coworkers. She also noted that it seemed like he had a lower tolerance for frustration.

In his research on relapse, he found that sometimes relapse is preceded by a feeling of overconfidence, being powerful, and especially of being arrogant. People also have a tendency to relapse when they stop living in the here and now and start ruminating about the regrets and resentments of the past. Perhaps most importantly, relapse is preceded by a need to isolate oneself, especially from the people who've been involved in your recovery.

John had gotten back in his support group and his men's accountability group. He did some of his research by questioning other people's experiences about what had led them to relapse. As he did his research, he once again realized the importance of people in recovery taking it one day at a time. So he made a commitment to himself, and to his support team, that as he would review his day each evening, he would make it a point to evaluate his "relapse possibility status."

STEP TEN

We continued to take personal inventory, and when we were wrong, promptly admitted it.

Step Ten is the first of three review steps. Steps One through Nine are the heart of the recovery program and process. First we dealt with our relationship with Jesus as our Higher Power, and the reality that we are powerless without him. Then we worked through Steps Four through Seven in order to know ourselves better, more deeply, and more honestly, and we asked God to remove our character defects. Then in Steps Eight and

Nine, we sought to make things right with everyone else in our lives. What more is there? Only to continue the process! Recovering from our addiction is a continual process that can last a lifetime. And Step Ten continues the path and the process of growing our knowledge of ourselves that began in Steps Four through Seven.

Working through Step Ten requires that we know where to work and where to look for the areas that need our attention. When we see patterns and frequent repetition in our behaviors, we realize that these are symptoms indicating that our recovery is lacking in some way. If we neglect or refuse to monitor our behavior, review artifacts, and make amends when necessary, we may have stopped our problem behaviors, but we have short-circuited our recovery and are not really living the life we could be.

The first principle of an ongoing and effective recovery is *honesty*. To be honest, we must embrace *transparency* and *authenticity*. We must give up the need to create illusions designed to convince people that things are not as they appear. We must refuse to allow our lives to be governed by fraud, double-dealing, or trickery. We work to root out any kind of deceit because we know that godly character has no need for deception. Proverbs 23:23 challenges us to "get the truth and never sell it." That includes the truth about ourselves.

Another area to review is the level of *striving* in all aspects of our lives. Are we striving to earn favor with God? Are we demanding of others because we are striving to achieve something beyond our capacity? Are we so perfectionistic that we exhaust ourselves trying to get everything just right so that we will look good and feel in total control? In our striving, we become pressured by what we think we "ought to do" and by what others tell us we ought to do. Life becomes a tyranny of "the shoulds," as we continually strive to do more, be more, or meet some incomprehensible demand. It never subsides.

Psalm 46:10 clearly tells us what God thinks about striving: "Cease *striving* and know that I am God" (NASB). When we stop trying to do things on our own, we renew our commitment to surrender.

This step is also written to remind us that we are human beings, that we will frequently be wrong. This step does not say *if* but *when* we are wrong. This also levels our pride and helps to keep us emotionally right.

This step also uses the word *promptly*, for the human tendency is to delay, delay, and then delay some more. We delay the recognition of our wrongs and faults. We also delay letting anyone know our wrongs. If we promptly admit and correct ourselves, we prevent these diseased thoughts from taking hold in our minds and hearts, and we can stay close to God. That's why James told us to confess our sins to one another (see James 5:16).

We must never give up, or think we have arrived, in our following of Step Ten. If we make it a habit to do a quick inventory daily, and promptly admit when we are wrong, it isn't that hard to stay on course. When we suffer, it's too easy to start grumbling and complaining and asking "why me?" We need to reject and reform that old habit. The admission of our faults and the willingness to correct our wrongs brings eternal rewards.

When we understand and deal with our own faults, then we become free to offer grace to others who need a break. Kindness, tenderness, and forgiveness are essential for a life of serenity. When our ongoing inventories reveal that we've strayed from the path of kindness, tenderness, and forgiveness, it's time to reassess our progress and do what we need to do to get back on track.

The apostle Paul warned: "If you think you are standing strong, be careful not to fall" (1 Corinthians 10:12). The best way to avoid falling is to take a regular inventory. And when we are wrong, humbly admit it and make it right.

QUESTIONS FOR STEP TEN

Setting Personal Boundaries *Genesis 31:45-55*

1. In order to restore trust in some of my relationships, what particular weaknesses do I need to set boundaries around?

_____

_____

_____

2. Is there a trusted person to whom I can clearly define my commitments? Who? What commitments am I willing to make?

_____

_____

_____

Weeding the Garden *Matthew 13:1-23*

1. While growing in recovery, some weeds will crop up in my life. How can I do a daily personal inventory to keep the weeds in check?

_____

_____

_____

2. What are some of the "weeds" in my life?

_____

_____

_____

3. How big is my addiction, or "weed"? (Maybe that's why I
   need a big God!)

_____

_____

_____

Repeated Forgiveness *Romans 5:3-5*

1. Do certain behaviors and character defects that show up
   in my Step Ten inventory point to a pattern? Which ones?
   What is being revealed?

_____

_____

_____

2. Am I having trouble admitting these properly in forgiving
   myself?

_____

_____

_____

3. Do I give myself grace? Why or why not?

_____

_____

_____

Be Angry and Don't Sin *Ephesians 4:26-27*

1. How have I experienced anger in my recovery?

_____

_____

_____

2. What is my first response when I am angry?

\
\
\

3. How was anger dealt with in my family? By my mother? By my father? Which pattern do I follow?

\
\
\

4. When I am angry, can I promptly admit it? Why or why not?

\
\
\

5. Do I have support people who can help me learn to deal with anger more appropriately? Do I have someone I can talk with about my anger? Am I willing to ask for help?

\
\
\

Spiritually Fit *1 Timothy 4:7-8*

1. Since this continual inventory is important for spiritual fitness, where in my daily routine can I set aside time to make self-assessment part of every day?

\
\
\

2. Do I have any resistance to evaluating my defects daily? What are my objections?

_____

_____

_____

3. Here's an example of a simple, daily, personal inventory:

Where have I been selfish, dishonest, fearful, or inconsiderate?

What have I done right today?

What do I need God's help with tomorrow?

What am I grateful for today?

_____

_____

_____

Looking in the Mirror *James 1:24-25*

1. Have I been quick to recognize but not to take action in a particular area of my life or ignore a defect of character? If so, can I take action without self-criticism by going back over Steps Six through Nine to work on that particular area or defect?

_____

_____

_____

2. In what area or in what defect do I need to take action today? This week? This month?

_____

_____

Recurrent Sins *1 John 1:8-10*

1. Have I hoped for immediate release from my defects? Have I personally or unknowingly hoped that by doing all the step work I could attain perfection? Write any thoughts and feelings that arise from reading this meditation.

_____

_____

_____

2. Is it clear that I still need inventories to continue my spiritual growth? Explain:

_____

_____

_____

3. Do I sense that my conscience is returning or developing so that I may always more easily recognize my faults? Am I humble enough to admit that more readily? Record any progress.

_____

_____

_____

Our lives require an ongoing evaluation
of our thoughts, deeds, desires, and motives.

PROFILE

Surrender allows you to grow as you submit to God's authority. In order to submit, you must trust that God has good things for you. His plans and purposes far outweigh what you bring to the table. There are times in our lives when it is very tough to believe that God has good plans in store. This was especially true for Jenny after her older brother was killed in a horrific head-on collision right as she started her summer vacation after her junior year in college.

Jenny struggled with her weight during this traumatic time. She unconsciously used food to soothe her cycling emotional state as she dealt with his passing. At the same time, she had no idea that her eating was connected to her emotional pain.

She also falsely believed that God could not be trusted because he didn't protect her family by preventing this tragedy from happening. God could not be trusted, so why would she submit to such an authority? The lie became so ingrained that she refused to date anyone. Marriage was not for her, for it meant having to submit to another person, and she wasn't about to submit to anyone.

She was disappointed with God and thought she could prevent bad things from happening if she managed everything in her life on her own. She figured the more she took charge of her life, the less chance she had to be hurt. She wasn't going to give control to anyone for fear of being hurt.

The heartache caused by this type of thinking could have all been avoided if she had recognized this lie. She had an inaccurate view of God based on her traumatic experience of loss. As a young adult, this prevented her from submitting her life to God's greater purposes, a step that could have saved her much grief. If she could have grasped the concept of surrender, she could have been free from her obsessions and experienced a better life.

In college, Jenny had struggled with her weight. She was a cheerleader and was extremely active. There were daily practices and gymnastic classes, in addition to the games. After road games, the team and the cheerleaders would stop at fast food places and load up on food. Her fellow cheerleaders ordered shakes, double burgers, and fries. Since she was thin and had just exercised vigorously, she figured she could load up on food and stay thin.

Well, she couldn't. In spite of all the exercise and activity, she began to gain weight. She was convinced her metabolism was slower than everyone else's. She had never had a problem with her weight before, and she was skinny as a kid while growing up. What she really needed to do was face reality. She was eating a whole lot more food on away-game nights, and her metabolism had little to do with her weight gain. It had more to do with regular late-night eating in the dorm. But for years she believed she suffered from a low metabolism rate.

As she grew to be able to accept her brother's death over the next couple years, she got her weight back under control, repaired her image of God, and got married. And along the way, she learned a lot about healthy eating.

STEP ELEVEN

We sought through prayer and meditation to improve our conscious contact with God, praying only for knowledge of his will for us and the power to carry it out.

Step Eleven is the next review step, in which we practice a new way of living and a new way of praying and meditating. It is a review of the first three steps in our journey. Those beginning steps had to do with getting our relationship right with Jesus Christ as our Higher Power and surrendering our lives to him. Steps Four through Nine helped us search our hearts and lives, make confession, and try to make restitution as best we could. In Step Ten, we began the process of reviewing our lives on a regular basis to keep ourselves on track. Step Eleven gives us our marching orders as we seek "through prayer and meditation to improve our conscious contact with God."

If we look back at our prayers, we often discover that they consist mainly of our asking God to deliver something we want. "Give me . . . forgive me . . . bless me . . . fix me . . . show me . . . protect me"—that about sums up the content of most of our prayers. We connect with God in order to get things from him for ourselves or for someone else. We forget about the source and become fixated on the results that he gives. Step Eleven invites us to move beyond our self-centered motivations into a godly desire to know God better and understand what he wants us to do with our lives.

As in every step, some key words make a huge difference. The first significant word is *sought*: "we sought . . . to improve our conscious contact with God." A relationship with God doesn't just happen. We must desire it, seek it, pursue it. Jesus promised that "Everyone who asks, receives. Everyone who seeks, finds. And to everyone who knocks, the door will be opened" (Luke 11:10). King David expresses this desire by praying, "The one thing I ask of the Lord—the thing I seek most—is to live in the house of the Lord all the days of my life, delighting in the Lord's perfections and meditating in his Temple" (Psalm 27:4). These are the words of a man seeking to improve his conscious contact with God.

Of course you will want to work this step through your process of dealing with your eating disorder. We want to get God's perspective on what we are doing. All too often we get stuck in our own perspective, get frustrated with God, and feel like he has abandoned us. To move forward in our recovery, it's important that this step become a way of life for us.

We can usually connect with God best when we have a place to step away from the hustle and bustle of life where we can commune with him privately in prayer. Yes, we can ask for things. But we also want to be sure to thank him, praise him, and wait quietly before him to allow him to light up our hearts, minds, and spirits. If we are having difficulty praying, we can use God's Word as a source of our prayers.

In some of Paul's letters to the churches, he includes written prayers for them. We can also pray these prayers for ourselves (see Ephesians 1:15-23; 2:16-21; Philippians 1:3-11; Colossians 1:9-14).

We can pray the Psalms as if they were coming from our own hearts. In a number of his psalms, David showed his struggles with his relationship with God. Note that David often complains in the first half of the psalm, but then he affirms his relationship with God in the last part of the song. It's a great model to follow.

What about meditation? The model for meditation is also found in the psalms: "I have hidden your word in my heart, that I might not sin against you" (Psalm 119:11). Hiding God's Word in our hearts is a form of meditation. Another example of someone hiding God's Word in her heart is Mary, who hid the words of the shepherds about Jesus in her heart and then "thought about them often" (Luke 2:19). Another translation (NIV) says she pondered what the shepherds said.

This step also directs us to pray for only two things. First, we must pray for the knowledge of God's will for us. In fact the step says to pray "*only* for knowledge of his will for us." The focus is on the here and now. Rather than asking God to fulfill our requests, we relinquish control of our lives to him. The shift makes God the focus, not us. His will is the purpose, direction, and the "why" of our lives.

The second thing we are to pray for is the power to carry

out God's will in our lives. The prophet Isaiah reminds us that God is the source of our strength: "Those who trust in the LORD will find new strength. They will soar high on wings like eagles. They will run and not grow weary. They will walk and not faint" (Isaiah 40:31). We all struggle with impatience. Now, we must learn to wait upon the Lord if we want to find new strength, especially when we are grieving.

Jeremiah also reminds us of a truth that he realized in the midst of his own grief: "The LORD is good to those who depend on him, to those who search for him" (Lamentations 3:25). It's important that we remember that God favors us, he is good to us, and he blesses us when we depend on him and when we search for him, which is an ongoing process. We can never get too much of God. We must never stop searching for all of his dimensions. Our challenge is to continue in prayer and meditation so that we grow closer to God and know more about his purpose for our lives.

QUESTIONS FOR **STEP ELEVEN**

Thirst for God *Psalm 27:1-6*

1. What am I seeking most from God?

\
\
\

2. What is most difficult about trusting God with my requests?

\
\
\

Joy in God's Presence *Psalm 65:1-4*

1. What keeps me from accepting and experiencing God's comfort?

_____

_____

_____

2. What scares me about the probability that God wants to redeem my eating disorder in some way?

_____

_____

_____

Finding God *Psalm 105:1-9*

1. Am I changing from day to day? Am I moving through the process? Identify some ways that things are changing.

_____

_____

_____

2. Am I becoming more aware of others' feelings and needs? What have I noticed today?

_____

_____

_____

3. Make a list of what you can thank God for today.

_____

_____

_____

Powerful Secrets Psalm 119:1-11; Luke 2:16-20

1. What Scriptures have I hidden in my heart in the midst of my recovery?

_____

_____

_____

2. Meditation means to ponder Scripture throughout the day. What has been easy about meditation? What has been difficult?

_____

_____

_____

3. Has meditation helped me? How?

_____

_____

_____

Patient Waiting Isaiah 40:28-31

1. How does impatience show itself in my recovery? In my relationship with God?

_____

_____

_____

2. Am I impatient about my progress in recovery? Do I expect perfection?

_____

_____

_____

3. Why is it hard for me to trust in the Lord?

_____

_____

_____

God Is for Me *Job 19:8-27*

1. In my working the steps, has God seemed like my enemy? In what ways?

_____

_____

_____

2. Am I tempted to do God's will in my own power? In what situations?

_____

_____

_____

Enjoying the Calm *Matthew 16:24-26; Galatians 6:9*

1. In what ways am I addicted to chaos?

_____

_____

_____

2. Why has chaos felt more comfortable for me than the calm of recovery?

_____

_____

_____

3. How does focusing on doing God's will introduce me to the calm?

_____

_____

_____

God is on our side,
even if we can't see it now.

PROFILE

Melinda had finally reached her goal—she had lost 119 pounds. You'd think she would be exuberant, but she was disappointed. Her disappointment stemmed from the fact that she was convinced that if she lost that much weight, her food issues would be behind her. She said, "I guess somewhere in my imagination I believed that if ever I lost this much weight again I would surely be floating from social event to social event, never daring to eat junk food or binge again. Life was going to be great!"

She found that for her, too many days were just as difficult as they were on the first day she started to lose weight. There are still some days when she makes poor choices about her eating and even falls off the wagon. And there are some days when she is tempted to go back to her old eating habits and just give up. She's found that changing her eating patterns and habits is just as hard today as it was at the beginning.

When she reviewed her notes from the New Life workshop that she attended, she found over and over again the words that "transformation comes through connection and community and practicing what you know works." So she shared her frustrations with her community, and even made an appointment to talk with her pastor. They all said basically the same thing to her.

What she learned was that she had a habit of letting go of God's hand, of moving back into her old pattern of self-sufficiency. They reminded her that it was not about the weight.

For her, it was about depending on God for everything in her life. Her goal is to enjoy good emotional health, good physical health, and good spiritual health. She needed this reminder, for she had forgotten the total picture and instead spent time focusing on the food addiction and her frustrations.

As she refocused, she found that her frustration level went down and her satisfaction level went up. She said, "My friends are truly a gift from God. They reminded me that I must do my part, but I must also allow God to do his part. And it truly is a journey taken one day at a time! I can't get ahead of myself."

STEP TWELVE

Having had a spiritual awakening as a result of these steps, we tried to carry this message to others and to practice these principles in all our affairs.

This step has three parts: First, we have had a spiritual awakening. Then, we are to carry this message to others. Finally, we are to practice these principles in all our affairs.

Let's look at the first part of this step—*Having had a spiritual awakening*. The Twelve Step recovery program is often called a selfish program. And in some ways it is. It has to be, if we are going to change. But those who work the first eleven steps find that when they come to Step Twelve, they have had a spiritual awakening. So it begins as a selfish program, but it becomes a spiritual program.

As soon as we find recovery, we want to share it with others. It's normal to want others to experience what we are experiencing. But we must temper that zeal realistically. It is too tempting to want to carry the message to others before we have lived the message ourselves. That's the reason this is reserved for Step Twelve. We don't begin recovery with Step Twelve; it comes after we work the first eleven steps. We work the steps this way so that we don't become instant authorities on something we haven't really experienced yet. If you haven't worked all the steps, you need to stop working on this step and go back to where you left off.

What does "spiritual awakening" mean? It is both a mystery and a miracle at the same time. A spiritual awakening could mean that over a period of time I begin to see God's hand in all that has happened. Connecting, praying, working the steps through the pain, and accepting the struggle as part of the process often draws a person closer to God and provides a spiritual awakening. Sometimes it's quick; other times it progresses slowly.

There is also a danger in thinking about a spiritual awakening as an event rather than a process. We may become discouraged if we do not experience a major or sudden shift in our emotions or thinking. But if we are open to the spiritual things of God, looking for God's hand in all that happens to us and moving toward God and not away from him, then we can be confident that we have begun the spiritual awakening. And when we are spiritually awake, we realize that others are not. This brings us to the second part of Step Twelve: *we tried to carry this message to others.*

Here is a story to illustrate this point: Once a man fell into a hole and began screaming for help to get out. A physician passed by and yelled into the hole that if the man could find a way out, he should come by the clinic and have his injuries treated. A lawyer came by and informed the man that he had a good case for a lawsuit, and if he ever got out of the hole, he should be sure to come by his office. A third man heard the cries and realized they came from his friend, so he jumped down into the hole with him. The man who had fallen in could not believe it. He told his friend he needed help getting out, not someone to jump into the hole with him. The friend replied, "Don't worry, I jumped down on purpose. I've fallen in the same hole myself, and I know how to get out." He then told the man to follow him, and he led his friend out of the dark hole.

This is what we need and what we need to do for others. We need help from those who have been in and gotten out of the dark hole where we find ourselves. And once we get out, we need to be willing to jump back into the hole so we can help others find a way out. When we have been healed, it is our turn to carry the message of hope to others. The apostle Paul said, "If another believer is overcome by some sin, you who are godly should gently and humbly help that person back onto the right path" (Galatians 6:1).

The third part of this step is *practicing these principles in all our affairs*. It's not easy, but it sums up a life of recovery. To practice the principles found in the Twelve Steps in all our affairs produces a life of serenity, purpose, and meaning. It creates a manageable lifestyle in which we find ourselves connected to God in a new and intimate way. And we are drawn to others like never before. Let's review the principles:

STEP ONE: *We must recognize our powerlessness in the unmanageability of our lives daily.*

STEP TWO: *God removes our insanity and restores our wholeness.*

STEP THREE: *We surrender to God and let go of control.*

STEPS FOUR AND FIVE: *We make an honest inventory of ourselves (not others) and share our confession with another person.*

STEPS SIX AND SEVEN: *In humility, we seek help from God to cleanse us and fill us with new strengths.*

STEPS EIGHT AND NINE: *We recognize the harm we have caused to others and take action to heal our damaged relationships.*

STEP TEN: *We continue to take inventory of our behavior, and when we are wrong, we promptly admit it.*

STEP ELEVEN: *We are increasingly more conscious of God's presence.*

STEP TWELVE: *We give away what we have gained in our journey through the steps and remain in recovery in every life situation.*

Practicing these principles is similar to what Jesus told his disciples: "Those who remain in me, and I in them, will produce much fruit. For apart from me you can do nothing" (John 15:5). We cannot practice the principles of the Twelve Steps without being connected to Jesus. Our priority is to apply the steps in any problem, event, situation, job, relationship, or loss—in other words, in anything that life brings to us—through the power of Jesus. When we connect to Jesus by deepening our conscious contact, he enables us to live more effectively, responsibly, and joyously.

Our shortsighted purposes for our lives begin to fade as we realize that with God's help, we can conquer anything. The miracle of this partnership with God is so awe-inspiring that we are encouraged to continue recovery no matter how arduous it may be. We realize that material, worldly success pales in comparison to living vitally and purposefully. The book titled *Twelve Steps and Twelve Traditions* of Alcoholics Anonymous states, "True ambition is not what we thought it was. True ambition is the deep desire to live usefully and walk humbly under the grace of God."*

---

* *Twelve Steps and Twelve Traditions* (New York: Alcoholics Anonymous Publishing, 1986), 124–125.

QUESTIONS FOR STEP TWELVE

Our Mission *Isaiah 61:1-3*

1. How have I progressed through the pain and despair of my addiction? How close am I to changing?

_____

_____

_____

2. Having had a "spiritual awakening" in working these steps, how can I share my experience with others?

_____

_____

_____

Our Story *Mark 16:14-18*

Write down the story of your spiritual awakening and how your recovery process contributed to the awakening. Describe how you have changed.

_____

_____

_____

_____

_____

_____

Persistent Prayer *Luke 11:5-10; Isaiah 52:6-7*

1. How has prayer changed for me since working the steps?

_____

_____

2. What makes it difficult for me to be persistent in my praying?

_____

_____

3. Have I become more interested in praying for others? Why or why not?

_____

_____

_____

Sharing Together *John 15:5-15*

1. Am I connected to the vine? How do the Twelve Steps help me to abide in Christ?

_____

_____

_____

2. How have the changes brought about by working the Twelve Steps made me more loving toward others?

_____

_____

_____

3. What am I doing to reach out to others with Jesus' love?

_____

_____

_____

Listening First *Acts 8:28-40*

1. What is my attitude about sharing my story of recovery? Am I reluctant to tell my story, or am I the kind of person who tends to share too much too soon with too many people?

_____

_____

_____

2. Am I willing to wait for God's timing for sharing my story?

_____

_____

_____

3. Do I see my story of recovery as valuable to God's plan for me? Describe how.

_____

_____

_____

Seeing Your Progress _1 Timothy 4:14-16_

Paul encourages Timothy to "throw yourself into your tasks so that everyone will see your progress." What changes in my life might others observe since I have been working the Twelve Steps?

_____

_____

_____

Never Forget _Titus 3:1-5_

What memories do I have about my old way of dealing with food? Are there any good memories? Describe some of the positive events that you want to remember.

_____

_____

_____

The Narrow Road *1 Peter 4:1-4*

1. In what ways have I suffered physically for Christ in my recovery process?

_____

_____

_____

2. What do I still fear?

_____

_____

_____

3. How can I work the Twelve Steps regarding this fear?

_____

_____

_____

CONCLUDING THOUGHTS

It has been our goal to help you with the recovery process in relation to your eating issues. We hope this process has been beneficial. We also wanted to use the Twelve Steps as a guide for dealing with your food addiction. The temptation now is to think that we have finished the Twelve Steps, but the truth is, we never finish because we never quit growing emotionally and spiritually. We've taken you through a path and a process that, with God's help, can guide you through any problem you might face. That's why it's called life recovery.

You will carry this message to others as you integrate the principles into your daily living. You don't have to boldly proclaim this message; you just need to live it. The message is carried further and better by a kind tongue than by articulate lips. So carry a message of hope and transformation as you love others with all you have and all you are.

Here is a blessing that we hope will be an encouragement to you from the apostle Peter:

> May God give you more and more grace and peace as you grow in your knowledge of God and Jesus our Lord. By his divine power, God has given us everything we need for living a godly life. We have received all of this by coming to know him, the one who called us to himself by means of his marvelous glory and excellence. And because of his glory and excellence, he has given us great and precious promises. These are the promises that enable you to share his divine nature and escape the world's corruption caused by human desires. In view of all this, make every effort to respond to God's promises. Supplement your faith with a

generous provision of moral excellence, and moral excellence with knowledge, and knowledge with self-control, and self-control with patient endurance, and patient endurance with godliness, and godliness with brotherly affection, and brotherly affection with love for everyone. (2 Peter 1:2-7)

Prayer for Recovery

Let me focus my will today on my eagerness to do the will of God through working the Twelve Steps and not to chase my evil desires or addiction.

SCRIPTURE INDEX

Isaiah 55:1-9 God's Abundant Pardon
Isaiah 57:12-19 Clearing the Mess
Isaiah 61:1-3 Our Mission
Jeremiah 18:1-6 Giving Up Control
Lamentations 3:17-26 God Is Faithful
Ezekiel 33:10-16 Hope for Those Making Amends
Daniel 4:19-33 Grandiose Thinking
Hosea 11:8-11 Covenant Love
Amos 7:7-8 The Plumb Line
Jonah 4:4-8 Going Deeper
Matthew 5:21-26 Handling Anger
Matthew 5:23-26 Peacemaking
Matthew 7:1-5 Finger-Pointing
Matthew 11:27-30 Submission and Rest
Matthew 13:1-23 Weeding the Garden
Matthew 16:24-26 Enjoying the Calm
Matthew 18:23-35 Forgiving Others, Forgiving Yourself
Mark 5:1-13 Internal Bondage
Mark 10:13-16 Like Little Children
Mark 16:14-18 Our Story
Luke 2:16-20 Powerful Secrets
Luke 8:43-48 Healing Faith
Luke 11:5-13 Pride Born of Hurt
Luke 11:5-10 Persistent Prayer
Luke 18:10-14 A Humble Heart
Luke 19:1-10 The Blessing of Giving
John 5:1-15 Discovering Hope
John 15:5-15 Sharing Together
Acts 8:28-40 Listening First
Acts 17:22-28 Discovering God
Romans 1:18-20 Believe
Romans 5:3-11 Rejoice Always
Romans 5:3-5 Repeated Forgiveness
Romans 8:35-39 An Overwhelming Struggle
2 Corinthians 2:5-8 Grace-Filled Living
2 Corinthians 4:7-10 The Paradox of Powerlessness
2 Corinthians 7:8-11 Constructive Sorrow
Galatians 6:9 Enjoying the Calm
Ephesians 2:8-10 A Clean Slate
Ephesians 4:26-27 Be Angry and Don't Sin
Philippians 2:5-9 An Open Book